A MAN ALONE

1st Edition

Published in 2012 by
Woodfield Publishing Ltd
Bognor Regis PO21 5EL England
www.woodfieldpublishing.co.uk

ISBN 978- 1-84683-142-3

Printed and bound in England

Cover photo: Bob Robinson in uniform,
shortly after returning from Burma.

A Man
Alone

The early life and wartime experiences of
Robert T. (Bob) Robinson *as a soldier of
the 14th 'Forgotten' Army in India & Burma
during World War II*

PETER COURT

Woodfield

Woodfield Publishing Ltd

Bognor Regis ~ West Sussex ~ England ~ PO21 5EL
tel 01243 821234 ~ e/m info@woodfieldpublishing.co.uk

Interesting and informative books on a variety of subjects

For full details of all our published titles, visit our website at
www.woodfieldpublishing.co.uk

To Jean Robinson, Bob's loving, kind and supportive wife, who, together with Bob, accepted me as a good friend in their home.

Bob Robinson shortly after returning from Burma.

"Important principles may, and must be inflexible."
Abraham Lincoln

"I can be on guard against my enemies
but God deliver me from my friends!'
Charlotte Brontë

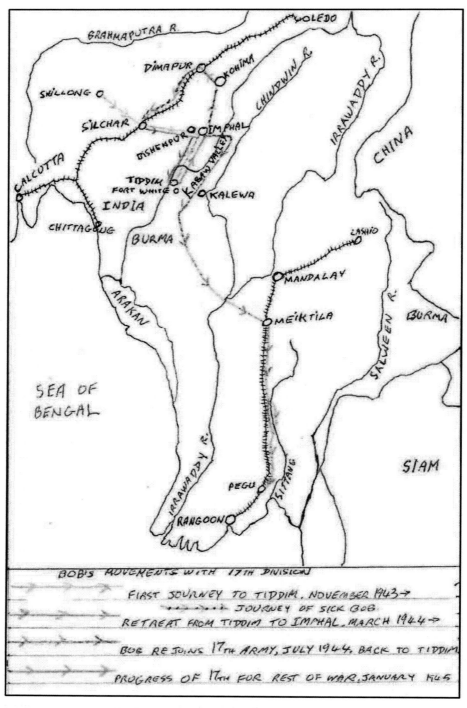

A sketch map of Bob's movements with 17th Division.

~ CONTENTS ~

Author's Preface iii

About the Author... vi

SCHOOL AGE.. 1
ASPATRIA 1
WINDERMERE.. 1
FIRST CONFRONTATION 2
KIRKBY- LONSDALE 3
THE TEN COMMANDMENTS 3
EARLY DISSENTION IN THE RANKS 3
POST SCHOOL YEARS.. 7
HEALTH AND STRENGTH MAGAZINE 8
WAR CLOUDS LOOM 9
DUNKIRK AND THE 13th COMMANDMENT............................ 12
THE PERFECT MAN 13
BOUND FOR THE EAST 15
FREETOWN... 16
AROUND AFRICA 17
FIRST SIGN OF DISHONESTY 19
IN INDIA... 20
THE CLIQUE 22
THE ORIENTATION RACE.. 23
SPORT AND GUARD DUTY AT FORT WILLIAM 25
PLEASURES IN CALCUTTA... 27
WALLET 28
A LOOK IN THE FACE OF DEATH... 28
THE HOOGLIE CANAL INCIDENT 29
DARJEELING 32
SHILLONG – TO BLOW A BRIDGE... 34
FIRST CONTACT WITH THE ENEMY... 36
PASSWORD 41
RETREAT 41
KOHIMA 46
CLEARING THE IMPHAL PLAIN.. 47
DISEASE AND HYGENE 51
BACK TO TIDDIM 53
IN PURSUIT.. 54
THE KABAW VALLEY... 57
TO CROSS A RIVER 61
ACROSS THE BURMA PLAINS 61
ACROSS THE IRRAWADDY 62
MAGGOTS 66
ANOTHER SNAKE ENCOUNTER.. 68

ON THE ROAD TO RANGOON.. 69
ELEPHANTS 69
DOGS AND VULTURES 71
A BREN-CARRIER INCIDENT 72
EXPLOSIVE DEMOTION...75
THE COMFORT OF TEA...79
LETTERS FROM HOME.. 80
ONE-TO-ONE STALKING 80
DEATH IN A VILLAGE 83
MONSOON SLAUGHTER 84
SLAUGHTER AT THE SITTANG RIVER 90
THE BURNING PYRE 92
JAPANESE PRISONERS 93
NO ROOM FOR CARELESSNESS 94
THE END OF THE WAR 96
HOME SWEET HOME 96
THE ORDINARY JAPANESE SOLDIER 100
THE CLIQUE AND BOB 100
BOB'S INJURED TOE...105
THE JAPANESE MILITARY PHILOSOPHY 106
LIEUTENANT JOHN PETTY 108

In Conclusion 109

Bob's Own Writing 111

FRIENDLY FIRE by Bob Robinson (written in 2002) 111
THE GOLDEN GRASS by Bob Robinson (2002) 114

Last Thoughts 118

Bibliography 120

Author's Preface

When I was four years old I was asleep in my bedroom in my parents' house on the Berea in Durban one night in 1945. I awoke at midnight to the sound of sirens and hooters going full blast all over Durban, especially from the many ships in Durban harbour. I called for my mother. When she came into my room I asked her: "What is all that noise?"

"The War is over!" she said.

"What's a war?" I asked.

Had the world retained innocence like mine at four years old it would be a better place today. It was not many years after that night, however, that I learned that my two uncles had been involved in that war, one of them as a pilot and the other as an aeroplane mechanic in the South African Air Force in North Africa and Italy. Both of them survived the war. I also found out that my doctor father was stationed at Lobatsi hospital in what was then the British Bechuanaland Protectorate (now Botswana) where he attended to sick Allied soldiers who were taken off the trains that travelled to the war in North Africa. Furthermore, I learned later that my grandfather and two of his brothers had been with volunteer South African troopers inside Ladysmith during the Siege of Ladysmith in 1899/1900. One of these brothers, William Gray, went on to take part in the First World War and was killed at the bloody Battle of Delville Wood on the Somme.

With so many of my family members having been to war, it was not surprising that I developed an interest in wars, or rather, in men who had participated in wars. Inspired by a short hand-written diary written by William's brother Lumley Gray of his experiences in the Siege of Ladysmith, I wrote my novel, Hear the Ringdove Call.

I immigrated to Vancouver in 1995. In 2008 I used to take my step son-in-law to work on Saturdays at a friend's house in West Vancouver. My step son-in-law had a couple of short conversations over the fence with Bob Robinson and learnt that Bob had fought as a British Infantryman against the Japanese in India and Burma in WWll. By then my uncles had passed on and I regretted that I had never gleaned from them enough about their war experiences in WWII to write about them. But here was a real live

World War II veteran within reach! I went to his house, introduced myself to him and told him I wanted to write a screenplay about his war experiences.

Bob was cautious at first. He said he had never really spoken about his experiences and on the very few occasions that he had referred briefly to them people were not interested in hearing about them. That was the first indication I got of why this has been called "the forgotten war." And yet in it Britain underwent its longest retreat in history and Japan suffered its biggest land defeat in history.

Well, I had now found an infantryman who had been in that war and it was a privilege for me to hear Bob's story. I visited Bob on Saturdays for several years, taking notes. In the end I decided that it would be better for me to write his story as a book rather than as a screenplay. Perhaps a screenplay could come later.

Field Marshal Sir William Slim and Lieutenant Colonel John Masters both said that an army can be seen as an inverted pyramid with the broad base at the top and the whole balanced on a single fine point – the will, skill, and discipline of the individual soldier. We are going to look at one of these individual soldiers.

In this book I deal with the following sections, all of which piece together the man, Bob Robinson:

(1) some of Bob's early life experiences, which help to determine what he would be like in later years
(2) a period of time in the army before he left England
(3) his journey to and training in India and his furlough time
(4) his actual war experiences
(5) problems that Bob experienced with some his own men during these war years

Lastly, I attempt to channel (1) to (5) towards a reasonable conclusion.

As we follow Bob's progress through the part of the war that played out in India and Burma, I occasionally describe briefly an event on some other part of the battlefront to clarify or broaden the picture of the whole army's progress.

For reasons that will become apparent later, apart from Bob's name, the only real names I use once Bob is in the army are those of some of the senior officers such as Field-Marshal Sir William Slim and Lieutenant Colonel John Petty. The only other real name I use is that of Bill Bell, who was in charge of transportation for Bob's regiment. I do use the correct names of some medical personnel and the names of some writers who participated in or wrote about the war.

This story is not intended to show any discrimination against any one group of soldiers who fought for our freedom. I have endeavoured to show the life of a soldier, particularly that of Bob Robinson, during this oft-forgotten but crucial part of World War II. I have on occasion given my own opinions on some matters but no person is bound to agree with those opinions when I offer them.

I hope that I have written this book in such a manner that anyone who knows little about World War II in India and Burma will be able to follow and appreciate the military events in this true story.

Peter Court

ABOUT THE AUTHOR

Peter R.G. Court was born in British Bechuanaland Protectorate (now Botswana) in 1941. His family moved to Durban, South Africa, when he was two years old. He completed his high school education at Durban High School in 1958 and a BA degree at Natal University in 1963. In 1964 he took a break from university and took part in Brickhill/Burke stage productions of Oklahoma and A Midsummer Night's Dream. In 1965 he completed his University Education Diploma and in 1966 a BA Honours degree in English, both at Natal University, Pietermaritzburg. During these years he was

an avid cricket and rugby player. Highlights were his selection in 1960 as a wing for the Natal under 20 rugby team and in 1962 for the South African University cricket team as an opening batsman.

From 1967 to 1977 he taught English at Alexandra Boys' High School, Durban High School and Glenwood Boy's High School. From 1978 to 1992 he lectured in English at the Durban College of Education (Durbanse Onderwys Kollege).

During his teaching years he had several poems published in literary magazines. Inspired by a short diary written by his great uncle about his time in Ladysmith during the siege of Ladysmith, Peter spent many years writing his novel, Hear The Ringdove Call, which was published in 2007.

In 1995 Peter emigrated to Vancouver, Canada, with his wife Louise. He has two daughters, Amanda, who lives with her family on a farm near Chesterfield, England and Jessica, who lives with her family in Johannesburg, South Africa. Peter has five grandchildren. He has written seven feature screenplays, set mostly in times of war, including screenplay versions of *Hear the Ringdove Call* and *A Man Alone*.

SCHOOL AGE

"In the end, every important battle develops to a point where there is no real control by senior commanders. Each soldier feels himself to be alone. The dominant feeling of the battlefield is loneliness."
Field Marshal Sir William Slim

Bob too, felt this loneliness when in action, but it was not the only loneliness that he felt during his time with the British Army. As the story unfolds, it becomes apparent that Bob Robinson experiences another form of loneliness: separation from his own men.

This story begins with seven-year old Bob, living with his family, namely his policeman father, John Aaron Robinson, his mother Margaret and his younger brothers, Stanley and little Eric, in the town of Aspatria, five miles from the western coast of England, in the county of Cumbria.

ASPATRIA

The word "Aspatria" means "St. Patrick's ash tree". *Ash* is the operative word because Aspatria in the 1920s and 1930s was part of an extensive coal mining area and Bob remembers the almost constant cloud of coal dust in the town. His mother's beautiful lace curtains soon became black with dust, no matter how often she washed them.

Bob remembers being taken down a coal mine on one occasion. Deep under the ground he saw pit ponies that never saw the light of day pulling coal trucks along narrow railway lines and blackened men shovelling the coal on to conveyor belts that dragged it upwards as though to blight the surface light – perhaps a suggestion of the war years to come.

WINDERMERE

Bob's father understood his wife's wish to move away from the daily gloom so, in the summer of 1930, the family moved away from the grimy, depressing coal mining areas of the west coast and their tall derricks and slag heaps. No one in that area travelled very far in those days and Bob used to think that England was one vast coal mine with everything under a fine layer of dust, only washed away when the rains came.

The short move to Windermere was like moving to a new country. What a change! The air was fresh and the smell of the countryside was everywhere. It was like a heaven on earth. They moved into a brand new house near the beauty of Lake Windermere, the largest mere in England.

FIRST CONFRONTATION

Early in his time in Windermere, when he was nine years old, Bob had an experience that gave some indication of what he would be like as a person and what his future would hold. He walked with his young brother, Stanley, into a mountain area to explore their new picturesque habitat. On some flat ground at the top of a hill they came across a group of about eight boys of a similar age to Bob. After a tense few moments of scrutiny, one of the boys walked up to Bob and blurted, "You're not allowed here!" and punched Bob. Bob was quick to reply likewise and knocked the boy onto the grass. Bob turned with Stanley and started walking away. One of the boys followed them and hit Bob on the back of the head with his pair of shoes with laces tied together. Bob stopped and turned. All eight of them were ready for action. Wisely, Bob turned and walked home with his brother. The boys did not follow. It was only later that Bob found out that the youths of nearby Bowness were in a constant feud with the youths of Windermere. He and Stanley had unwittingly strayed into enemy territory.

I believe that this little incident gave some indication of things to come. Bob was faced with a crisis that he had to deal with alone; his brother was too young to fight. I believe this incident was also the start of Bob's becoming a loner. I do not mean that in a negative sense; he was defending his brother as well as himself but had to act alone to do it. He was starting to develop an independence that would stand him in good stead but which would also set him apart from others, a position that others would not necessarily admire. It was also an early indication of Bob's physical strength and of strength of character.

Bob's father, John, was a policeman and, like Bob, was very much a man who preferred to function on his own. He was not happy that his superintendent in the department was always looking over his shoulder, so he applied for a position in a smaller town, where he was likely to have no superior officer. As a result, the family stay at Windermere lasted not much more than a year.

KIRKBY- LONSDALE

In the summer of 1931, when Bob was ten, his family settled in Kirby-Lonsdale, where the country atmosphere proved even better than at Windermere. Bob loved the history attached to the town. There was a Norman church close to his house, parts of it dating back to the Norman conquest in 1066. A walk through the churchyard led to "Ruskin's View" of the River Lune. The Victorian poet, John Ruskin, expressed admiration of this view as depicted in a famous painting by J.M.W. Turner (1775-1851). Beyond the river were fields full of cattle and sheep. A farmhouse nearby was centuries old with a watchtower still intact. In the background were the fells, with their miles of dry-stone walls and trees everywhere and all so green.

Still there, half a mile downstream, is the 'Devil's Bridge' a single-lane bridge built 700 years ago. Parts of an old Roman road are still in the area, so is a small Druid's circle, probably dating back 3,000 years.

THE TEN COMMANDMENTS

It was at this time that Bob heard the local Anglican priest preach about the Ten Commandments. Bob thought here was a structure for his life's path. It was as simple as that. He would try to lead his life accordingly from that day on.

He must have talked to his father about the Ten Commandments because he remembers his father telling him, "That's good, Bob, but you must also learn to look after yourself. Nobody else will." One could say that this became Bob's eleventh commandment.

The opportunity to live by this new commandment came sooner than young Bob expected.

EARLY DISSENTION IN THE RANKS

A new town meant a new school for young Bob. The school was built in the year 1850 and it was said that in 1650 Oliver Cromwell marched with his soldiers along the road in front of the school on his way to do battle with the army of Charles the 1st – perhaps another hint of battles to come.

Bob had hardly settled in at the local elementary school when one day he found himself shoved up against a stone wall by a big strong boy with red hair and wearing the usual farmer's son clothing of a rough corduroy shirt and trousers. With a smirk on his face, the big lad bunched the front of Bob's shirt in his hands and held him against the wall while another lad, slightly taller and slimmer than the first, stood calmly to one side. Bob had time to notice the second lad's smart breeches, leggings and shirt – the clothing of the son of a country squire. The smart boy did the talking.

"So it's Bob is it? Well Bob, I am Tom Clark. All the boys here do what I say. If they don't, they suffer at the hands of Tom Atkinson here." To instil the point, Tom Atkinson gave Bob a hard slap across the face and an even harder couple of punches in the chest.

Just then, the school bell rang to signal the end of recession. Tom Atkinson released Bob, who flopped to the ground. He remained there, partly stunned, while all the boys ran past him on their noisy way back to their classrooms. Bob did not cry. When he entered his classroom, a lesson was in progress. His cheek was swollen and red.

"New boy Robinson," the teacher said. "You'll have to do better than this. Fighting at lunch break and late for afternoon class? Do that again and you'll be punished. Take your seat."

He found the looks of pity in the eyes of his classmates as he walked to his seat far worse than the pummelling he had just taken. Bullying was new to Bob; he had not encountered anything like it at his earlier schools. He kept out of the way of the two bullying Toms.

Boys in his class told him that on most afternoons many kids would play a casual game of football on the school field, so the next day he walked alongside the school field to watch the game.

Smart Tom Clark was standing idly on the sideline, watching the game while Big Tom Atkinson was in the thick of the action on the field. On one occasion he tripped a boy to get the ball to himself, then dribbled it towards the goal, where he scored.

All those on his side cheered loudly.

Clark shouted, "That's three to none! Get on with the kick-off side B."

Side B kicked off from the centre mark and the game was in progress again. Very soon big Tom Atkinson had the ball in his possession again. At one point he overran the ball and another boy kicked it away.

"Stop the play!" Clark shouted. "Townsend, come here!"

All was immediately quiet and the boy who kicked the ball walked part of the way towards Clark, then stopped.

"You tripped Atkinson!"

"N-no, Clark, he accidently bumped me," stuttered Townsend.

"Liar!"

All the boys were now in a ring around Townsend. Atkinson stepped into the ring and gave Townsend a savage punch. The boy fell down. Atkinson then gave him a kick.

"That's enough," Clark commanded from the sideline. "A free kick to side A!"

The kick was taken and the game moved off to another part of the field. Townsend remained on the ground, groaning. Soon he arose and limped off the field. Bob took an involuntary step towards him but noticed Clark looking his way, so he stopped, turned and walked home.

Bob just had to find an answer. He could think of nothing else. He wanted revenge and to prove to the school that he was not a coward. In the meantime, he took a passive role in school activities.

Bob knew that the man next door owned a small gym in town and the following day he asked the man's permission to use it. When he got there he found a gymnastics class in progress. He joined the group and was soon a budding gymnast. After every lesson or session he would go to an old, battered punchbag that was anchored to the floor in the corner and pound the bag with both fists as hard as he could for about twenty minutes. His gym instructor would, from time to time, watch him then walk away, muttering and shaking his head. He would occasionally inspect Bob's hands and ask why he was not using the special gloves provided. Bob did not give him his reason.

Within a year, Bob won the gymnastic championship for his age group. But after every practice he always finished by pounding that punchbag. He never had any boxing lessons; he just punched and punched the bag as hard as he could.

He also ran by himself. Every afternoon or evening he would put on his running shorts and shoes and off he'd go. He ran in the streets, he ran in the countryside, he ran all along the fell racing courses; every day he ran.

A year after his fateful meeting with the two Toms, at the age of twelve, Bob was as fit as anyone could be and brimming with confidence. He decided he was ready to confront the bullies. He went to school that day, determined, resolute. He told himself he would fight all day and night if necessary; no matter how much he got beaten, he would press on, he would never give up.

The usual soccer game started on the playing field after school and Atkinson took up his usual domination of the game while Clark took up his idle command post on the sideline. When the game had been in progress for about ten minutes, Bob appeared from the school buildings in his running shorts and shoes and trotted past Clark. Clark raised his eyebrows.

Bob joined the side opposing Atkinson. Everyone was caught by surprise when Bob seemed to appear from nowhere, rob Atkinson of the ball and set off in the opposite direction. At first there was total silence as all other players stood still. Then...

"That's a foul! Foul play!" Clark shouted from the sideline.

Bob just carried on with his solo run with the ball at his feet. Atkinson recovered from his surprise and pursued Bob as fast as he could, closely followed by all the other players, now yelling in excitement. When Bob began to get near the goal, Atkinson mouthed obscenities at him and yelled, "Someone stop that soppy sissy!"

Bob immediately stopped and turned to face Atkinson.

"*You* stop me!" he said.

Atkinson pulled up, more surprised than ever. All the players arrived and breathlessly formed a circle around the two boys. Even the few lads watching from the sideline ran onto the pitch to swell the circle – all except Tom Clark. Atkinson leered at the smaller Bob. Bob just stood, straight-faced. The ring of boys was absolutely silent.

Atkinson went for Bob with arms flailing. Bob struck with his right fist. It went between Atkinson's arms and made contact with his cheekbone below his left eye. He stopped as though pole-axed and collapsed to the ground. Bob felt but ignored a searing pain in his knuckles. There was a huge whispered "Wow!" from the boys. Atkinson sat up and looked at Bob with a hand on his left cheekbone. Bob waited and waited. But Atkinson would not get up.

The ring of boys made way for Bob then followed him as he left the circle and walked towards Tom Clark. Bob stood close to Clark and looked at him. Silence.

Clark looked at Bob for a minute then turned and walked away. There was no more bullying at the school after that.

While walking in town one day, Bob heard his name being called. The gym instructor was with some of the locals. He said, "Hey Bob, I saw the town bully today. He had a big black eye and a bruised face. Do you know how it happened?"

Bob just grinned. The instructor's face broke into a smile and he mouthed, "Wow!"

The building of the old school is now about 180 years old and has been turned into flats. The playing field, the scene of Bob's victory, is today covered in houses.

In 1984 Bob visited an old school friend in Kirby Lonsdale, who had been one of the boy witnesses of the fight. They recalled the incident and laughed about it. But it was no laughing matter at the time.

POST SCHOOL YEARS

Bob left school when he was 14 years old. His father didn't approve but Bob was adamant. He had always wanted to become a carpenter. At home as a kid he made some of his own toys out of wood – a horse cart, a little farm house with wooden fences and sheds, a racing cart, a small table. No woodwork lessons were given at his school; he taught himself as he went along.

When a boy left school in that area in those days there were only two jobs available, farm labourer or miner; neither appealed to Bob. He was lucky to land a job as a general helper on a wealthy man's estate where new animal sheds and tenant cottages were being built. He started as a fetch, carry and tidy-up boy but was soon helping with the woodwork.

His exercising did not end either. He joined the local .22 rifle club and soon became a proficient marksman. In 1938 he took the club championship trophy away from a man who had been the champion for three years. With the trophy he received an invitation to enter the annual shooting competition at Bisley but with no transport or money available to him, he could not attend. He borrowed his father's shotgun from time to time, went out into the countryside and stalked and shot rabbits. It is difficult to do this: wild rabbits are alert, sensitive creatures. Without knowing it, this shooting and stalking was a good preparation for his later war years.

Bob kept up his running too; at night and in the day when he had the chance. He ran mainly in the countryside and always alone.

One Saturday Bob was running along a public path when he came to a crossway. Many people were walking along the path that crossed his path.

He stopped to let them pass but became curious as to where they were heading. So he followed them. Soon they came to a rugby field where a game was in progress. He stayed and watched the game. The crowd applauded when a man brought off a good tackle and again when another scored a spectacular try. The more he watched, the more he became fascinated by the game. All he wanted from then on was to join the local rugby team. When he was 15, he joined Kirby Lonsdale Rugby Union Football Club.

At 15 years old Bob was five feet four inches tall and weighed 110 pounds. When his parents saw him in his rugby jersey for the first time, the hem was down to his knees. His father could not stop laughing but his mother said, "What? Are you going to play with all those big men?"

And big men they were. Little Bob got knocked around a lot in the game. But he played on the wing because of his speed and he scored some good tries. Nobody really taught him how to play. He asked some fellow players questions but mostly he figured the game out for himself as he went along. He was carried off the field a few times but usually managed to return before the game ended. One Saturday he was concussed and did not wake up until Monday. He lost a couple of teeth too. He says that visits to the doctor and dentist must have cost his father a lot but he never complained. In fact, his father watched most of the games. Bob loved the game and continued to play whenever he could.

In the summer he played cricket and became a useful pace bowler.

Bob also took part in fell running in the area. The 'fells' of Northern England are open, hilly countryside. Fell running includes a significant component of gradient climbing, so runners must possess mountain navigation skills and carry adequate survival equipment as prescribed by the organizer. There could be a choice of routes to take between checkpoints. All this activity amounted to a very fit young Bob.

HEALTH AND STRENGTH MAGAZINE

Health and Strength magazine was first published in 1894. Bob obtained a couple of copies before the war. The magazine and the Health and Strength League, which was formed in 1906, pursued all aspects of physical culture and had as their motto: "Sacred thy Body even as thy Soul." This phrase inspired Bob. One could say it became his 12th Commandment, which he endeavoured to follow all his life.

In 2011, at the age of 92, Bob attended the local gym in West Vancouver three times a week and played golf twice a week.

WAR CLOUDS LOOM

On 1st September 1939 the Germans attacked Poland and the following day Britain and her allies declared war on Germany. Soon men were joining the army all over the country. When Bob walked home from work through town one day, a couple of old men standing on the veranda of a pub shouted loudly at him.

"Hey Bob! When are you going to join up?" Everyone in the street stopped and looked at Bob. The following day the same thing happened. The same old men shouted: "When are you going to join up Bob? We were in the trenches when we were your age." Again, people in the street stopped and looked at him as he walked home.

Bob would not be goaded into doing something he did not want to do. He knew their rude bravado was a form of showing off, yet I believe these incidents added to the layers of solo determination within him. He did join up but not because of these loudmouths – he had heard his father talking about the German threat and had listened to the crackling family wireless.

By 1939 Britain had registered 270,000 territorials, the part time volunteer force of the British army, although they could be called up for full time duty at any time. Bob joined the Cumbrian territorials, at that time called the 50th Northumbrian Division. They were whisked off to the west coast of Cumbria to patrol the coast and guard against any possible German invasion. So as a young soldier Bob found himself once again amongst the coalmines, slag heaps and grimy conditions.

He remembers his group being driven to a drill hall for their first training. They were in a large covered truck that was badly ventilated. Fumes came up into the enclosure and all the men were sick and dizzy when they arrived. It took them half a day to recover. He wondered at first if this was a preparation for gas warfare. In summer the men were housed in tents and in winter in converted cow sheds. Welcome to the Army!

Duties included guarding up to 200 rail trucks, many of them loaded with high explosives intended for the war effort. These were parked on sidings that extended on either side of the main line. As a young lance corporal Bob found himself with so much responsibility that he got very little sleep. By morning he was asleep on his feet.

The guardroom was a railway coach. The guard Commander, a First World War veteran sergeant, knew how to avoid work. So Bob had to mount sentries every two hours, try to find them in the pitch dark among all those rail trucks and check them continuously to see that they were doing their job. Occasionally he'd find two struggling figures and realize that one of them was a girl from the town. He would give the man a stern warning not to do it again. It often took several minutes to find the man's rifle. In WW1, Bob reasoned, the man would probably have been shot for "neglect of duty."

The cookhouse/dining room was built of railway sleepers. It had a dirt floor but it was snug and warm. Food and a cup of tea did wonders. The officer would come around to see Bob at some time during the night but, in the dark, the pouring rain and a howling wind, his visit was brief. Bob, however, had little respite. The trees shook and bent in the wind and all kinds of strange noises and moving shadows made Bob imagine strange things such as enemy agents in the dark planting limpet mines on the sides of the trucks or someone sneaking up behind him and whacking him over the head.

Luckily the men's long gas capes kept them dry and broke the wind. But the biggest comfort of all was their rifles, which, if they survived, never left their sides for six and a half years.

They cordoned off the beach areas and planted mines in preparation for a possible German invasion. Every night German bombers would fly over, following the coastline on their way to specific targets. Before long Bob would hear the distant thud of exploding bombs.

An occasional fighter plane would follow the railway lines, looking for targets. They passed over the soldiers' heads. Thank goodness they did not know what was below! On one occasion a sentry shouted, "You bastard!" and raised his rifle to fire at a plane overhead. The old sergeant grabbed the rifle and with a shout of "You idiot!" knocked the startled young man to the ground. A shot would have made the pilot realize that there was something worth shooting at down there – and 200 rail trucks full of high explosives would have made quite a bang!

On two occasions Bob was with troops, well away from the rail trucks, when a fighter plane appeared from the south and swooped down on them. The men scattered and dived for what little cover they could find. The plane gave a burst of machine gun fire, then flew away. Luckily, nobody was hit.

Bob was issued uniform and clothing by a quartermaster in Kendall. He could see that the seam at the back of one boot was defective. He asked the quartermaster to change his boots but the man just bawled him out in front of other soldiers and would not change them. For a long time Bob's foot got wet.

Bob admits that he was eager and innocent in those days and seemed often to be pushed into doing things that nobody else wanted to do. One example was when his and a couple of other platoons were sent up a long, arduous climb to the top of a hill in order to clean a pile of billycans and pots at a campground. When they arrived at their destination, they found a big pile of the filthy, greasy billycans beside an old mess building. They looked around the area but could find no taps or any source of water nor cleaning utensils.

The men wondered what to do. Then they saw an officer emerge from the mess building some twenty yards away. All the men urged Bob to ask the officer how they were expected to do their cleaning job. Bob agreed and, like a lamb to the slaughter, approached the officer. Bob was surprised to see that the officer was the same quartermaster who had issued him with the defective boots. He asked the officer how the group were going to clean the billycans without water or utensils. The officer eyed Bob steadily and, with a boot, dug up a lump of dirt. Then, keeping his eyes on Bob, he dumped the lump of soil into Bob's quickly outstretched hands.

"With that!" the officer said as well as a list of profane terms. Then he turned on his heels and entered the building.

And that is just what the men did. They spent hours cleaning every can by scraping them with dirt. Luckily, they were also able to find a small water tap to aid the process.

Bob got bawled out yet again when the old WW1 sergeant was supposed to wake him up for his two-hour shift on guard duty one night. The sergeant did not wake Bob, who overslept. When he reported to the officer in charge, who should the man be but the same quartermaster! Not only was

Bob bawled out, he was also confined to barracks for five days, including a weekend. The old sergeant was considered immune to blame.

Poetic justice of a sort occurred later. That particular officer was known not only for his screaming at soldiers but also for his dandy way of dressing. His hair was always combed and greased perfectly. His uniform, and in fact all his clothing, was always neat and tidy. At times he even added an extra touch, perhaps pinning an extra unearned medal on his chest at a parade or an army function. He went too far when, at a military dance, he arrived wearing a splendid police chief's uniform. He thought he would be the highest ranking officer at the dance but a little later the RSM (Regimental Sergeant Major) arrived and bawled at him in front of all the guests and soldiers, saying, "Get out of that monkey suit!"

DUNKIRK AND THE 13th COMMANDMENT

Early in May, 1940, Bob kept up his rugby by playing in an army rugby game. He was heavily tackled and kicked in the groin so badly that he had to undergo an operation and spend a couple of weeks in hospital. It was while in hospital that he was told that his unit had been sent to France with the British Expeditionary Force (BEF). He was upset, thinking that his chance to serve his country in action had passed, but he was soon to hear that the Germans had pushed the BEF and thousands of French troops into a small pocket on the French coast around Dunkirk.

From 27th May the evacuation of troops from Dunkirk began and, against all odds, 338,226 men were rescued, including 141,842 French soldiers. By 4th June 1940 the evacuation of Dunkirk was over. Six out of every seven men from the British Expeditionary Force had been rescued. However, these did not include the men from Bob's D Company. He learnt that in a disastrous engagement, his entire unit had been killed, wounded or taken prisoner. It was a long time before their relatives heard what had happened to them. Bob had grown up with and been at school with some of these men. Most of them were from the Kendal area, where Bob's parents now lived. For three months Kendal became known in the newspapers as "The Town of Missing Men." Missing the chance to go to France had probably saved Bob's life.

Many years after the war, Bob visited Windermere, hoping to find a lad he had sat beside in school when he was ten years old who later had been in Bob's first regiment. The first thing Bob did was to visit the war memorial in the town and the first name he saw was that of his school companion.

For Bob it was back to patrolling the North West Coast. It was at about this time that Bob heard Churchill's inspiring speech on a radio in the Camp. The Germans had swept aside all opposition thus far. They were in control of Europe. They were going to attack England. There was silence, no motion in the Camp as though time stood still as Churchill's calm, imposing voice rallied not only the British but the whole free world.

"We shall defend our island, whatever the cost, we shall fight on the beaches, we shall fight on the landing grounds, we shall fight in the fields and in the streets, we shall fight in the hills; we shall never surrender...." (4th June 1940)

Bob was inspired. This speech bolstered his sense of purpose in life. His home town priest's words and his policeman father's early words gave him a structure; live your life according to the Ten Commandments but also look after yourself, because no-one else will. In this time of national need, Churchill's words now added patriotism to this structure – a love of country and a determination to serve it – a 13th commandment, one could say. It would not be too long before he would have to try to obey that commandment too.

THE PERFECT MAN

Back on the northwest English coast, Bob's accommodation took a step up from tents and converted cattle sheds; he was billeted with other soldiers in a building that had been a drill hall during WW1. It overlooked a sports field. One morning Bob looked from a window at the sports field down below. He saw several men trotting around the track and others chatting on the starting line of the one hundred yard sprint. He put on his running shorts and shoes and went down to the track to see whether the army had an athletics club or whether he could at least join the men there in their training.

When he arrived on the track he saw a tall, well-built, good-looking athletic man pace out a ten yard start for one of the other men at the 100 yard starting point. Then the man returned to the proper starting line and readied himself for the race. One of the bystanders stood as judge at the finish line while another took the role of starter and gave a loud: "Ready, steady, go!" The two of them were off in a sprint to the finish line. The tall athlete surged past the other runner and won comfortably. He then walked back to the starting line, where he challenged a second man to a race with a ten yard start. Again the tall athlete won easily. Then a third man took up the challenge – with the same result!

When the tall man came back to the starting line, his breathing was almost normal, as if he had not just run three hundred yard races. This time he took a breather and told Bob and a couple of other men standing at the line that his name was Brian Bentley and that before joining the army he had been a professional soccer player. He talked on about some of the matches and athletic events in which he had excelled.

When he had stopped talking, he gestured at the track and said: "Would anyone else like to challenge me?"

Bob stepped forward. Brian Bentley looked at short Bob and smiled.

"All right. Get to that ten yard start."

Bob did so and, at the given signal, off he sprinted. To Brian Bentley's dismay Bob won by about five yards.

"Well, after three races already..." Brian Bentley said, "But we'll do it again. Back to the start."

He and Bob walked slowly back to the start, breathing evenly.

"This time you get only five yards start," Brian said, as he measured out Bob's new starting point.

Off they went again. This time Brian managed to get within a yard of Bob but still lost the race. He refused to let the situation go and told Bob to run a third race.

The two of them walked back slowly to the start once again, where Brian measured out a two yard start for Bob. When they both said they were ready, off they went again.

This time Brian managed to beat Bob by about one yard.

As both men breathed heavily to recover, Brian said, "I would easily have beaten you the first time if I had not had sex with seven women last night."

Actually, he used far more profane words. He then walked off the track.

One of the bystanders then told Bob that Brian Bentley was disliked by his fellow soldiers for being a boaster and a womaniser, even a marriage-breaker

Bob did not come across Brian Bentley again until military training in India, where he soon learnt that Bentley had made himself popular with senior officers in the army. He spent time drinking with them in their mess. He represented the army in soccer matches and athletic events in India throughout the war. Every time his group was about to be sent to the front, he developed "feet" trouble and stayed behind. The last Bob heard about Bentley was that at the end of the war he went home with syphilis.

BOUND FOR THE EAST

Bob was not destined to spend the rest of the war patrolling the northwest English coast. He was called up to go much further away. He was assigned to the Headquarter Company, 9th Infantry Battalion, Border Regiment, part of the 17th Indian Division in the British 14th Army. The 17th Indian Division, sometimes called the 'Black Cat' Division because of its insignia of a black cat, had been fighting the Japanese in Burma from the start of the Japanese invasion of that country in December 1941. With appalling losses, the British were pushed back over the border with India. The Japanese had conquered all of Burma by the end of April 1942. British, Indian and Gurkha casualties were 10,036, of which 3,670 were killed. This was the longest fighting retreat in British Army history – 1,350 miles over five months. The Burmese army had 3,400 casualties and the RAF lost 116 aircraft.[1]

There was then a pause in the war, as the British prepared themselves for a push back into Burma and the Japanese prepared for the invasion of India. This lull in the fighting was at about the time that Bob left England.

Bob and his fellow soldiers boarded the transport ship, the *Orcades I*, which left Liverpool as part of a large convoy of 24 ships in May 1942, accompanied by two battleships, HMS *Nelson* and HMS *Rodney*, the aircraft carrier *Illustrious* and six destroyers. In peacetime the *Orcades I* had been the flagship of the White Star line. Even when stripped down as a troop carrier she was beautiful. The convoy travelled around the north of Ireland and then into the Atlantic. Bob recalls that once into the Atlantic the presence of all these warships gave one a great sense of security.

German submarines shadowed the convoy but were kept at bay by the destroyers. Bob was leaning over the rail when the first alarm was raised. Immediately four of the destroyers turned and raced off to two locations and began to drop depth charges. This was almost a daily occurrence.

---

[1] Chris Trueman www.historysite.co.uk The Retreat in Burma.

Because of the danger presented by submarines, the convoy went a long way off course, almost to the coast of North America before turning east and heading for the coast of Africa.

This was young Bob's first time at sea and the Atlantic can get pretty rough. The rolling of the ship bothered Bob the most. After two days he went down with seasickness. What followed was a bit of a nightmare. Besides the seasickness, half the people on board went down with food poisoning. The proud *Orcades I* began to take on the appearance of a hospital ship. The passageways were full of soldiers desperately trying to find a bathroom. Others were draped over the railings while many were just curled up on the decks. There were queues trying to see the doctors who were working overtime. The doctors did a great job because no-one died. But what a week!

Since this infantry regiment's history dated back hundreds of years, the daily training continued for these men. For a period of time each day the soldiers were marched ten abreast round and round on the promenade deck. On the second day the ship's Captain complained that the continual regular pounding of boots vibrated down to the engine rooms and was slowly but surely destroying his ship. From that moment on the men still marched – but out of step.

FREETOWN

Bob felt relief when the convoy finally sailed into Freetown, the capital of Sierra Leone on the west coast of Africa. Thanks to the Royal Navy, the convoy did not lose a single ship. The harbour was at that time, apparently, the third largest in the world. There were approximately 100 capital ships at anchor there, including many warships – an impressive sight.

The forbidding-looking dark-green jungle came right down to and hung over the water's edge. There were no beaches or flat areas to be seen other than the large flat area on which Freetown stood, the tin roofs of its buildings gleaming in the bright sun.

Freetown was also a base for the RAF, whose Sunderland Flying Boats were patrolling the coast, on the lookout for enemy ships and submarines.

The *Orcades I* stayed for six days, taking on fresh water. No-one was allowed ashore. In fact, the ship was anchored at quite a distance from the shore, to be out of reach of malaria-carrying mosquitoes. The area was known as "The White Man's Graveyard" due to the frequency with which European visitors were struck down with malaria and other tropical diseases.

The men on board found the atmosphere humid and oppressive. There wasn't the slightest movement of air. Perspiration drenched their bodies. Sleep was almost impossible. You finally dozed off through sheer exhaustion. In the near future they were to experience similar conditions in India and Burma, where heatstroke really took its toll and those badly affected by it would not recover.

Happier events were visits from the natives, who paddled out to the convoy ships in their flat-bottomed boats and did a brisk trade selling fruit and leather goods. Money was let down in baskets and goods hauled up the same way. Others stood up almost naked in the boats and if you threw down enough silver coins, they would dive into the water, swim underneath the huge ship and pop up on the other side – an incredible feat.

AROUND AFRICA

The *Orcades I* left Freetown in a smaller convoy which sailed down the coast of West Africa and around the Cape of Good Hope. Bob remembers seeing the *Queen Mary*, also converted into a troopship, sailing in the opposite direction, heading back to England, probably carrying Australian and New Zealand soldiers. The men were amazed that she had no escort. They were informed that because of her speed she was out of reach of the submarines. Her appearance seemed like a good omen.

The convoy arrived in Durban on 4th July 1942. This time the men were allowed to disembark and stayed in a military encampment at Clairwood, on the southern side of Durban. Bob remembers that they slept in army bell tents and went swimming at nearby Isipingo.

This part of Bob's journey has its own "Jaws" story. The men were warned not to swim beyond or around a certain batch of rocks where a river entered the sea, disgorging its debris – an area known to abound in sharks. The ship's regimental barber did go around the rocks, however, probably dragged by the current – and was never seen again.

Bob and his men now boarded *The Empire Trooper*, a captured German steamship used by the British as a troopship.

As the *Orcades I* made its return trip to England it was torpedoed and sunk by a German U-boat 280 miles northwest of Cape Town. It took six torpedoes to send her to the bottom. When Bob heard the news he thought: "That is my second lucky escape."

Bob's photo of Clairwood Camp near Durban, South Africa.

Bob's photo of Isipingo beach, Durban, South Africa.

FIRST SIGN OF DISHONESTY

Bob was made platoon sergeant before leaving England for the East. Something happened on this stretch of the journey that began to make Bob realize that the men of his platoon did not necessarily share the same "Churchillian" concepts as did he. He was sitting on a hatch top on the deck, with his haversack at his feet, splicing the end of a two metre length of rope with which each soldier had been issued. The rope would come in handy, for instance, to secure a rolled up groundsheet and other objects or for building a shelter or for climbing. Bob was using a good knife with a shiny six-inch blade and a solid carved handle that his father had given him to cut free the strong tape that bound the three strands together at the rope end. He put the knife down beside him on the hatch cover and with his hands skilfully made an eye splice on one end of the rope. One of his platoon men, McGuire, watched Bob doing this then asked Bob to do the same thing to his rope. Bob agreed and soon several of the men lined up for the same purpose. Each time he finished slitting the tape from the rope end, he placed the knife beside him and continued the splicing with both hands. When he'd finished doing the last rope, he groped with his hand for the knife beside him. Then he turned and looked for it. It was not there. He stood up and looked around. Other soldiers were walking casually around the deck or leaning against the side rails looking out to sea. Nobody was taking any notice of him.

"Does anyone have my knife?" he asked politely but loudly. "It was right here on the hatch cover."

A couple of the men looked his way. One of them shrugged. The others took no notice. He never saw his knife again.

IN INDIA

Bob and his men disembarked at Bombay but there was no time for sightseeing. Bob was ordered with his platoon to unload the ship. All day and most of the night they toiled in the heat, directing huge slings down into the musty holds and attaching large equipment and boxes onto them. There was no respite. Not even a mug of tea. Absolutely worn out, they got onto a train that took three days to get to Calcutta. They had to sleep on the floors of the train coaches. Bob managed to sleep on a bench. When they woke up the next morning, cockroaches were running all over their bodies. They shouted and jumped up, brushing the creatures off, whereupon the cockroaches all ran down the crude toilet.

They were housed in military barracks at Fort William, which was built around 1781 by Robert Clive and covers an area of 70.9 hectares. For the first few days the men had to again sleep on the floor. When they woke up they were again covered in cockroaches. When the men stood up, the creatures, as in the train, all ran down the toilets. Bob also remembers that when the men finished eating in the mess and went out, a host of small cockroaches would appear and eat up all the crumbs.

'Oh well,' Bob thought, 'at least there's no waste.'

Bob remembers there being so many baboons around that area that one had to be careful to watch one's food. If you carried a plate of food across open ground, they would approach and pester you. The only way you could elude them was to throw bunched up brown paper at them, which they would investigate while you made your escape.

Another hazard was the kites that sat in numbers on the roofs. If you walked along with a plate of food on a tray, a kite was bound to swoop down and take the food clean off your tray. A few men got their own back by tying a chicken leg with a thin rope and attaching the other end to a brick on the tray. A kite would swoop down, take the chicken piece in its claws, take off then suddenly find itself dragged down to the ground. Efforts to take off again met with the same setbacks, much to the amusement of the men.

Bob's photo of the entrance to Fort William.

Bob also found himself the butt of the men's humour one day when a knock came at his door. He opened it to find a large cobra coiled up at his feet. Half its head was missing but even in death it could give one a nasty fright. 'Such was the sense of humour of the British soldier,' Bob told me.

While Bob was at Fort William, the Japanese bombed Calcutta on Christmas Eve 1942, a few times, indicating their intention to invade India. More air raids followed and thousands of inhabitants left the city.

On a more soldierly note, on the first trip to the shooting range where the men practised firing with .303 Lee Enfield rifles, Bob aimed at his target and fired the required amount of shots. Similar shooting exercises followed frequently. Bob was never told what his score was on that first exercise but from the second exercise onwards, on arrival he was told abruptly, "You do the instructing." His shooting experience back in England had clearly been valuable – and, of course, as a sergeant he had enough rank to do the job.

THE CLIQUE

During this time Bob noticed that, in his own section of the platoon, two men named McGuire and Merton and a few others kept together in a *clique*. Fred Merton was a big, strong man and seemed the most popular. Bob spoke from time to time with men in other sections who seemed reasonably good chaps but he made no real friends in his own section. Perhaps he felt his authority as platoon leader would be compromised if he did not keep himself slightly apart from the other men.

One day Bob entered his barrack room to find that the clique of about six men were sitting in a rough circle on their bunks. Their conversation came to an abrupt end as he entered. They all looked at him silently. Bob nodded at the men but received no nods in return. The men started some idle chatter for a couple of minutes, then Fred stood up and walked past Bob, who was standing to one side away from the door opening. As Fred drew level with Bob he stopped, smiled broadly at Bob and said, almost in an off-hand way, "Are you a Catholic?"

"No," Bob answered. "I'm Church of England. Anglican. But I seldom go to church. Why do you ask?"

Fred was walking out and did not answer. McGuire followed Fred and also paused beside Bob.

"We're all Catholics here," he said.

And with that McGuire left the room.

"Why should that matter?' Bob addressed the others.

A couple of them shrugged and one of them muttered, "No matter. No matter at all."

Greg Hadley, a blond lad of nineteen, was the next to stand up and begin to walk out.

"Your rifle, Greg," Bob said.

Greg stopped and looked at Bob.

"You're on sentry duty."

"I'm going to church. It's Sunday."

"It's your turn."

"But not on Sundays."

"You don't expect others to do your duties for you, do you?"

Greg looked at Bob then back at the others. Then he sighed, went to his bunk, picked up his rifle and went out. The other men returned to some idle talking, then, one by one, they stood up and walked out. The last one, Reg Walker, paused at the door.

"Going to church," he said with a smile.

Bob was left alone in the room.

Bob was not originally part of this section of the platoon but when he was appointed sergeant of the whole platoon he was also given this particular section as his "home" section. He soon realized that this section had made themselves a comfortable nest, as it were, and had wanted their own man, Corporal Fred Merton, to be the sergeant. So from the start, in their eyes, he was an intruder.

THE ORIENTATION RACE

The feeling of being on his own did not only come to Bob from below, it also came from above. The following incident illustrates this point. The soldiers from several groups were called to an area near the barracks that had been set up as a track for an orientation course, which was to include a group compass-reading race. Bob was the only man from his platoon and was put with a group of non-commissioned men, mostly non-combatants. Officers headed several other teams. There was no leader for Bob's group.

"Anyone the leader here?" Bob asked.

No answer.

"Who would you like to lead this team?"

Again no answer. Some shook their heads.

"Okay I'll do the job," Bob said.

The men simply stood still.

"All right men," Bob said, "Fall in."

The men looked resentful but formed up.

"Quick march," Bob ordered.

The unwilling bunch moved off. Bob learnt later that the men were all NCOs, non-military men who had signed up for the course, thinking they would have an easy couple of days.

Bob led the men to the track. The groups huddled together at a starting line, where an officer handed out race instructions and a compass to the leader of each team and barked out some of the rules. The general idea was that when the pistol was fired each team had to establish from the instructions and use of the compass to find where their first flag was hidden. Each group had a different coloured flag to find. Once a team found their first flag they were to tick off the first block in a sheet on their leader's clipboard then set off to locate the second flag, and so on. An officer would be concealed near each flag to ensure there would be no "crooking".

"Anyone done this before?" Bob asked his men.

"No Sarge," said one man said and the others shrugged their shoulders.

The starter fired the pistol and each group studied the instructions and their compass and set off at a trot. An officer in a group beside Bob shoved Bob to one side and shouted, "Get out of my way! Move over!"

Bob and his group were pushed further astray by two more officers leading groups. So he and his group went off-course, overran their first target and had to retrace their steps in order to find their first flag, then work out where to find the second flag. The result was that Bob's was one of the last teams to finish the course.

"What a bloody waste of time!" one of the men muttered and walked off the course.

Bob remained behind to listen to the organizing officer talking to some of the other leaders and clarifying some of the rules. Then Bob walked off, studying his list of instructions for the second race that was scheduled for the following day. When the men of Bob's platoon were fast asleep in their bunks that night, Bob was still studying the sheet with a small flashlight.

The next day saw all the groups gathered at the starting line for the next race.

Bob's group stood a short way behind the others in a huddle as Bob talked earnestly to them and pointed out details on the list on the clipboard. One man held the compass and nodded his understanding. Bob then said to his men, "This time we are going to show them what we ordinary soldiers can do."

The whistle blew for the groups to line up at the starting line. The officer in charge lifted his pistol and fired. Bob's compass man ascertained quickly the first target spot and the group set off at a run ahead of the other groups. They went straight to their first flag under a bush in the countryside of rolling hills and bush. They lifted the bush leaves to reveal the flag.

"Here it is!"

Bob ticked the item off on his list.

"Next one. Take these readings."

The compass man worked on the compass while the rest crowded around him. In no time the group was off running again. They were well on their way.

Bob and his group arrived at the finish line, a white line drawn in a flat grassy area beside two wood-and-iron shacks. No one was there.

Bob went and looked inside the two sheds. Empty.

He went back to the finish line. His men were resting in the shade of some trees at the side of the course.

"Maybe the whole army has gone back to England and left us here – got rid of us," one man said. The others laughed.

Just then a truck came through a gap in the surrounding trees and stopped near Bob. The starting officer got out and came up to Bob with his clipboard.

"Now then, what are you lot loafing around here for?" he asked.

"We've finished the second compass-reading race, Sir," Bob answered.

The officer looked incredulously at Bob and then at his stopwatch.

"What? Nobody could finish in this time."

"We did Sir."

The officer's eyes widened.

"You are a liar. You are a cheat!"

Bob was flabbergasted. He opened his mouth but could not get any words out. Then he managed to say, "No Sir! Here on my clipboard are our entries..."

But the officer turned and walked towards the second and third groups that were crossing the finish line. He approached those leaders and began writing down their details.

Bob looked at his men by the side of the course. They had heard but they said nothing. They just stood up and walked away. Some were laughing.

SPORT AND GUARD DUTY AT FORT WILLIAM

Sport, such as soccer and athletics, was organized from time to time between the rigorous training periods. Bob remembers one of the track meetings in which he represented his company. First, he took part in the 100-yard sprint. The runners took up their starting positions. The pistol sounded with a crack and they were off! The runners were pretty much in a straight line for the first 25 yards but then Bob, the shortest runner, surged ahead and won by five yards. An official ran up to him and recorded his details. The men who came second and third were joined by and congratulated by men from their own units. None of Bob's men came to him. The same situation occurred at the end of the 220-yard race and the 440-yard race, both won by Bob. To add insult to injury, Bob's prize was twenty cigarettes for each race he had won. And he was a non-smoker! He gave them to men in his platoon.

This disregard of Bob by his own men seems at first baffling. We know that Bob in his pre-war years was something of a "loner". He tended to keep to himself at school. When he was confronted by problems such as bullies he devised plans and dealt with them by himself. For years he trained in the gym and ran by himself. He joined a rugby club and played rugby with men much older than he was. He joined a shooting club whose members were much older than he was. If he attended any social activities of these clubs he did not drink and he did not smoke and did neither all his life. Even when his rugby team travelled by bus to other areas, the rest of the team drank beer after the game but young Bob did not. He would have a ginger ale and wait for the others on or near the bus. Men in the army are not likely to warm to a man who keeps largely to himself, who appears to them as "straight-laced", too good, and who does not drink or smoke. He did not share the usual infantryman's sense of humour, which was quite often laced with bawdiness or practical jokes.

Another athletics event of note was the Bengal Olympic Sports Meeting in Calcutta. Bob was chosen with three other men to represent the 9th Battalion in the 4 x 100-yard relay race. Other regiments took part as well as Indian civilian athletes from different parts of India. The 9th won the race. The four medals were kept by the army and after the war were donated to the Carlisle Military museum. The infamous Brian Bentley was not one of the team. Bob never learnt why but guessed it was one of those occasions when he had "feet" problems.

One night, Bob was on guard/sentry duty at the gates of the military base. His fellow guard for the night was not from his platoon. He was a good-looking young man who hardly left the guard hut the whole shift, unlike Bob who did his quota of patrolling along the fence from time to time. Bob had hung his army coat on a hook in the guardhouse. In one of the pockets was a good flashlight that Bob had found to be very useful.

When the shift was over the other guard left the area quickly. When Bob put on his army coat, the flashlight was gone.

A couple of days later, Bob noticed that the culprit was away from his barrack. Bob nipped into the empty barrack, sifted through the man's bag and found his flashlight. He pocketed it and never had anything more to do with the culprit. Bob had almost come to expect such incidents. But worse was to come.

PLEASURES IN CALCUTTA

During a couple of day's leave, Bob's transport co-ordinator friend Brian Bell took Bob to town in Calcutta. The two of them sat at a street café and sipped tea. To Bob's surprise, he saw Fred, McGuire and Jeff across the busy street. They were haggling with an Indian man. On the wall behind them were life-sized pictures of Indian women in traditional dress but with bare arms, lower legs and stomachs and breasts partly exposed. A real woman then appeared at the man's side and then Bob realized that the place was a brothel and that his men were bargaining for a price for the woman. A price seemed to be agreed, money exchanged hands and Fred walked inside the building with the woman. McGuire and Jeff laughed and walked a short way down the street and stopped at a similar shop where the same procedure took place.

"They're all married men," Bob said to Bill Bell.

The purity of Bob's view of this incident of whoring by men of his platoon is another thing that made Bob "a man alone." Sexual contact with women, mainly prostitutes, has been part of soldier activity since time immemorial, and British soldiers are no exception. An indication of this is seen in Ken Cooper's book *The Little Men,* when the adjutant gleefully tells Ken that their platoon will be leaving Burma to go to Calcutta and says, "Next stop, the Indian fleshpots!"

Venereal disease for the British army in WW2 was highest in the 14th "Forgotten" Army in India and Burma. In fact, in 1943 the rate of infection at any given time for that army was 158 for every 1,000 men.[2]

This moral goodness of Bob the soldier reminds us of his early determination to live his life according to the Ten Commandments. It is quite remarkable that he was still on that path during the war. It was natural for

---

[2] King and A. J. Strong: Medicine 1880 Churchman Publishing, Worthington.

him to think that this was the way people should run their lives. To me it does not reveal the attitude of a self-righteous prude, as some of the men in his platoon must have viewed him. "If you don't drink alcohol, don't smoke and don't go looking for women when you're on leave then you're not one of the boys, you're not one of us", the men in his platoon must have thought. I believe this is why they disliked him. The fact that he was made their sergeant increased their dislike. I'll go further and suggest that it is possible that the contradiction between their churchgoing and their whoring engendered a little guilt within them that was increased when seen beside Bob's abstinence. So they reacted with further dislike. The fact that Bob was not one of the boys in the other club, namely, they were all Catholics and he was not, increased the gap between them even further and in their eyes excused their actions against him. But a blameless man cannot be attacked openly, not even verbally, when he is your sergeant. Hence the covert, underhand tactics on which they decided.

WALLET

Another unpleasant incident took place in Fort William. After a day's training the men all took a shower in the barracks shower room. Bob was the last to enter the room. The other men were either finishing their showers or getting changed back into uniforms. Bob chose an empty spot on the shelves beside the showers. As he completed his undressing he slipped his wallet under his neat pile of clothes. He took his bar of soap and had a good refreshing shower.

When he had dried himself all the other men had left the shower room. He slipped a hand under the clothing. The wallet was not there. He checked again and went through all the pockets of his clothes. Nothing. There had been a few men from other platoons in the shower room so he could not be absolutely certain that the thief was from his platoon. However, he felt sure it was one of his men.

A LOOK IN THE FACE OF DEATH

On a day off while in Calcutta, Bill Bell, the army transport co-ordinator who Bob met occasionally, took Bob for a ride in a truck into the country-side to get away from army life for a few hours. At one stage in the trip, they went along a four-foot wide track in open countryside dotted with a few bushes. They stopped on a bridge over a small river. Bill took a couple of photos of the river from the bridge. Bob told Bill he wanted to get a close-up look at the river. He decided to leave his rifle in the truck. He walked to the end of the bridge, found a path that seemed to be going toward the river and followed it.

When he had walked about twenty yards, he saw what looked like a thick, yellowish stick lying across the pathway. When he got close to it he froze. He moved his eyes and head slowly to the left and saw that, sticking above a four foot clump of grass, was the yellow and black-edged face and hood of a King cobra staring into his eyes, a mere three feet away from him. Bob kept absolutely still, then backed slowly up the pathway. When he was several feet away from the snake it dropped behind the clump of grass and the part of it lying across the pathway vanished. Bob beat a hasty retreat to the truck and resolved never to leave a truck again without his rifle.

A King cobra can reach 18 feet in length and can raise one third of its length straight up off the ground and still move forward to attack. That was Bob's third lucky escape.

THE HOOGLIE CANAL INCIDENT

Calcutta is built on the banks of the Hooglie River. Many canals and ditches take the flow of water off the land and deposit them into the river. The canals and ditches are also used as convenient garbage dumps. Some of the canals are quite deep, especially in the monsoon season. The soil is like grey clay; in the dry season it is like concrete but in the wet season it is very muddy and slippery. Bob's platoon was out on a manoeuvre one day during the monsoon season. They had trekked all day across the country-side and had to cross a canal, then move through a bushy area then meet up with a truck that would take them to another part of the exercise – all to be done within a time limit. Bob led his platoon to the canal, where a single, wide plank, supported by a few poles, was the only way over. He noticed that the water looked deep and was flowing quite quickly. He stepped aside and motioned his men to cross before him.

When he was half way across he heard shouting coming from the bank he had just left. A couple of Indian villagers were running along the bank in a downstream direction towards the narrow plank. They were pointing frantically at something in the water. Bob saw a floating toupee approaching the plank-bridge. When the toupee was almost under him, it rose up and revealed the head of a gasping man and then he saw the flailing arms break water. Although he was carrying heavy gear on his back Bob got down on his knees and tried to grasp the man, but to no avail. The man was swept under the narrow bridge and further downstream, letting out a scream as he went.

"Someone get him out!" Bob shouted at his men, who were lined up on the opposite bank. They just looked on with curiosity. Not one of them said a word, so Bob took off his backpack and rifle, placed them on the plank, jumped straight into the water and swam after the stricken man. In no time he came alongside the man, who then flailed at Bob's face and grabbed his collar. Both of them went down. Bob swallowed muddy water but managed to surface and haul the man up. Then, with one arm clasped around the man's neck, he swam as best he could to the bank, where the man's friends jumped into the shallows. They took their man from Bob and dragged him onto the bank.

It was only then that a tired Bob realized that there was quite a strong current because it pulled him back to midstream. He struck out as hard as he could for the opposite shore but by now his clothes and boots were helping the current to pull him under. He looked frantically at the shore where his men had been standing.

"Men! Where're you?"

There was no-one there. The men had gone. It took Bob every bit of his remaining strength to keep his head above water as the current took him further downstream. Just when he thought he would drown, something smacked across his face. He found himself holding onto a thin rope stretched across the surface to a stunted tree on each side of the canal. He pulled himself gradually to the side then clawed and crawled his way onto the bank. He rolled over and lay there, panting, as the dirty water drained off him.

When he had gathered his strength and breath, he stood up, collected his backpack and rifle and walked into the bushy area to find the spot where the truck would be. He broke through the bushes onto a wide grassy area. The truck was there and all his men were seated on its open back, talking idly to each other. The motor was running and the Indian driver sat quietly behind the steering wheel. A red-faced field adjutant stood beside the front passenger door, holding a clipboard in one hand and the other one curled in a fist on his waist. Bob marched up to the officer and saluted. Before Bob could say anything the officer blurted: "Good God! Sergeant Robinson, you look a mess .What the devil have you been up to?"

"I jumped into the canal Sir, to save..."

"Just get a move on! You're way behind schedule. Get cracking to the next exercise point."

The field adjutant turned and walked off. As Bob climbed in, he heard a few sniggers from the back of the truck.

So it had come to an attempt on his life! Bob was stunned by the event and kept it all to himself. He decided that the men of the platoon had resolved to get him out of the way by awaiting an occasion when he would be in a predicament and they would do nothing to help him but would come away from the situation blameless.

The company was preparing to go to the front so Bob thought that he could not bother the authorities with accusations that he could not prove. All he knew was that he could never trust his own men again and that he had just had a fourth lucky escape.

Bob's photo of Tolly's Nulla, – one of the canals that flow into the Hooglie River.

DARJEELING

Bob's company did their training at and near Fort William for seven months, after which they were taken by train 388 miles north of Calcutta to a hill station at Darjeeling in Nepal. This was where the Colonial English used to retire for holidays, away from the heat and moisture of the cities. Darjeeling is 8,482 feet (2,133 metres) above sea level.

From the town of Siliguri the railway line zigzags and loops on its way to Darjeeling. In a distance of 51 miles it gains 7,000 feet. Bob recalls the amazing scenery and the many hillside tea plantations. The jungle area around Darjeeling is also tiger country. Although Bob's men never saw one, they knew they were there.

Darjeeling.

While at Darjeeling, Bob's group were given two weeks' leave. Bob was keen to go on a trip further up the mountains, so he asked several of the men if they would join him and they all said they would go with him. Bob went to the only hiking company in the town and booked five carriers or "coolies" and food and other requirements for a seven-day trek. The day before the departure date, all the men informed him they would not go.

A rather desperate Bob heard that his company's first lieutenant, Lieutenant J. Petty, had arrived the previous day, so he informed the lieutenant of his plight. Lt Petty said, "I'll go with you," and that was a great relief and the start of a wonderful experience for Bob.

The magnificent scenery, including views of Mount Everest and the mountain air, invigorated Bob. The highest point they reached was Sandakpan, 11,929 feet above sea level. Here are Bob's words:

"We viewed the vast snowy Himalaya range that has no parallel the world over in height, magnitude and extensiveness."

For Bob it was an uplifting experience, an elevated calm, before the descent to the bedrock of training and war experience.

Bob and Lieutenant Petty outside a Tibetan hut.

Back at their Darjeeling camp, Bob's company was put through strenuous Chindit-type training, which included exhausting marches through jungle and hilly countryside, sometimes as much as 30 miles in a day. They were being prepared for war.

At one of their last training courses they were shown some chilling photos so that they would have no illusions about the enemy they were up against. They were Japanese-taken photos. One was of a captured Allied airman on his knees with his hands tied behind his back with barbed wire, about to be beheaded by a swordsman. Another was of a Chinese prisoner being used for bayonet practice by Japanese soldiers. Another showed

Chinese prisoners buried up to their necks on a field while Japanese soldiers galloped on horseback about the field playing a game like polo.

Bob's photo of a camp site during a break in training.

SHILLONG – TO BLOW A BRIDGE

In July 1943 the brigade was moved to Shillong, about 250 miles to the west of the Imphal Plain. In addition to being a training area, Shillong was selected as a convalescence base for Allied troops because of its mild weather and relative accessibility from Imphal. More training was the order of the day for Bob's regiment.

One day Bob's platoon were given an exercise to do in the countryside. They had to march along a certain route and use a map and a compass to find a certain river. Having found the river, they then had to find a particular wooden bridge across the river and Bob, as the sergeant would have to devise a means of blowing up the bridge.

He was not to actually damage the bridge, however, because it served villagers on both sides of the river, but he had to prepare a means of blowing the bridge and an officer accompanying the platoon would give a report on his performance to senior officers upon returning to base camp.

By the time Bob's platoon had reached the required bridge the men were pretty spent but they had to hide behind a raised bank some fifty feet from the bridge. Bob produced a canvas sack he had brought containing packs of gelignite, four empty cans that he had obtained from the kitchen at base, a small roll of fuse wire and a cigarette lighter he had borrowed from the cook. He filled each can with gelignite and cut a suitable short length of fuse wire, which he inserted into the gelignite of each can. He put the cans carefully back into the canvas bag and crawled towards the bridge. He had to pretend that this was happening in wartime conditions. His men were supposed to be lining the bank on their bellies, ready to provide Bob with covering fire if he were to be discovered by the "enemy" and had to beat a hasty retreat.

Bob reached his end of the bridge on his knees. He waited until he heard the "all clear" – a pre-arranged birdcall from one of the men on the bank – then crawled to the middle of the bridge. He pulled the cans from his bag and placed them on the planks. He flicked the cigarette lighter on. At that point he was supposed to pretend to light the fuses and beat a hasty retreat back to his men on the bank. However, he noticed that there were gaps between the planks of the bridge floor that were wide enough for the cans to fit through. So he decided to make the "make-believe" exercise a bit more realistic. He deftly lit the ends of the fuses that were equidistant from their gelignite surfaces in the cans. He was taking the chance of injuring or killing himself if he pushed the tins through the gaps too late. Well, he managed to time it just right. He dropped the cans between the gaps in the boards, got up and ran towards his bank.

The cans of gelignite exploded beneath the surface almost simultaneously, causing an eruption at the surface. The exercise was no longer an exercise; all the men, including the officer, came running from the bank to the bridge and stared at the still bubbling water beneath it. Villagers from both sides of the river also came running down to the water. And when the bubbling ceased, fish began to pop to the surface, belly-up. The villagers shouted at each other. Some waded into the water to grab fish. Others ran back to their villagers to get boats so that they could collect the haul.

The officer was a lenient man. He gave Bob a stern warning for risking his life, praised him for feeding the local population and gave him a good report on the exercise.

FIRST CONTACT WITH THE ENEMY

In November 1943 Bob's group went by truck to Imphal and then all the way down the Imphal Plain to a town named Tiddim, just inside the Burma border. They then trekked by foot up many a high hill until they reached the town of Fort White. They also spent time at Kennedy Peak, which is just under 9,000 feet above sea level. Here they did more training.

The only way to get water up the mountains was by carrying galvanized drums up the pathways. Some Burmese "coolies" were used for this purpose. On one occasion Bob could see that there were not enough of these labourers to take the drums up a particular section of the mountain. Bob had always wanted to do things by himself so he attached two ends of his rifle belt to a drum, placed the loop across his forehead and took the barrel up on his back. As far as he can remember, none of his men emulated his task. In fact, he recalls them "melting away" when he set about his task. Perhaps as sergeant he should have asked a couple of the men to do what he was doing. When I put the question to him he replied that at that stage he mistrusted his men so much that he preferred to keep a distance between them, to order them to do only that which was essential.

Bob and a companion working outside a basha.

The hillsides were covered in vegetation in which it was easy to get lost. The footpaths had been made by natives over centuries. It was drilled into the soldiers that they were never to go off track alone or without an organized outing. They were told of an officer who, before their arrival, had wandered off into the jungle on his own and got hopelessly lost. Organised searches could not find him. Somehow he managed to survive in the jungle for about ten days and then, by pure chance, staggered into his base camp, a physical and mental wreck. He had completely lost his mind and never recovered.

Bob's platoon at mile 12 from Tiddim.

In March 1944 the Japanese began their attack into India with the intention of sweeping the British off the Imphal Plain and then to have the whole of India at their mercy. At first, small groups went well ahead of their army.

At this time an incident took place that puzzled Bob and shook his confidence a little. On this occasion he saw his first Japanese soldier and it was nearly his last. His platoon accompanied an officer and a second platoon on an excursion through a bushy area. One man was carrying a Bren gun. Two scouts went ahead as they moved along and astride a rough track for about an hour.

When the scouts returned and reported that the area ahead seemed to be clear, the officer ordered a halt for a breather. The man carrying the Bren gun looked sick and was attended to by a medic and the officer. After a few minutes the officer turned to Bob, who was standing nearby, and said, "Sergeant Robinson, take the Bren gun and go with Private Wilks back along the track. The scouts say all is clear for a mile or so but you two can go as a second probe."

Bob told the officer that he had not fired a Bren gun for a long time; it had been included very briefly in his early training, and he asked if he could take it a short distance to their rear to test fire it. The officer denied the request and walked away. Private Wilks from the second platoon was armed with a rifle. The two of them set off. Bob was only really happy with his rifle but orders are orders.

They walked carefully along the rough track for about forty minutes and Bob found the Bren gun to be rather heavy and clumsy. A Bren gun is a light machine gun, usually mounted on a Bren Carrier for mobility, or set on the ground, supported by a bipod and fired like a heavy machine gun. However, a Bren gun can be held by one man and fired from the waist during a charge or forward attack but seldom on a reconnoitring outing.

As they entered a clearing, they came suddenly across a lone Japanese soldier carrying a bag and moving across their pathway. Both parties were startled. Bob held the Bren in the general direction of the Jap and kept his finger flat on the trigger but it fired only a single shot that went wide. By then the Jap had dropped his bag and brought his rifle up into firing position.

"Blam!" The Jap soldier crumpled to the ground.

Private Wilks was a shade quicker.

Bob and Wilks checked that the Jap was dead then looked carefully around the immediate area but there was no other sign of the enemy. The Jap's bag contained rice. Bob and Wilks went back to the group and reported to the officer. Bob does not remember the officer showing much concern and shortly thereafter the group returned to camp.

Having hardly handled a Bren before, Bob did not see that the weapon was set on single shot mode. Bob puzzled over the officer's decision to send him on this move with a Bren gun but he was more thankful that Private Wilks was quick to react. Bob regarded this as his fifth lucky break.

The job of Bob's platoon was now for a while to find and dislodge small enemy groups that had occupied hills between Fort White and Tiddim. The platoon would work its way carefully up a hill. On some occasions they crept up a hill to find no traces of the enemy and on others they'd find traces of small fireplaces where the enemy had been but were now gone. Moving in the countryside and up and down the hills was tough going as each man carried a full pack.

It was on one such outing that another incident occurred that made Bob wonder more about his men's loyalty. They were going in single file as usual up a narrow pathway. Bob was in front. As his section moved in a semi-circle along a pathway on the side of a slope, Bob looked back. The men were carrying their rifles "at the trail", meaning that each man held his rifle at his side in his right hand at the point of balance. On this occasion the end of every barrel was pointed at Bob. Then in the next moment each one moved to its natural position in relation to the position of its bearer. Bob showed no reaction but turned his head forward again and carried on walking as normal.

A quiet man was behind him and McGuire was in third place. McGuire had been perspiring and complaining about the heat for some time. Then Bob heard the sound of someone tripping and falling behind him, followed by a rifle shot and then immediately by a scream. He swung around to find that McGuire had tripped and fallen and in so doing his gun had discharged and the bullet had hit the back of the arm of the quiet man immediately behind Bob. Both Bob and Corporal Fred berated McGuire for his carelessness. He had a half sheepish, half sullen look on his face, perhaps even a trace of guilt. Luckily it was just a flesh wound. The quiet man's arm was bandaged and strapped up by the medic and he was sent back to base with a helper.

The patrol went on as usual but Bob couldn't help wondering about the incident. Was it really an accident caused by carelessness? They had trained and trained and marched endlessly in that type of terrain before the move to Tiddim. The men were all fit and deemed ready for front line soldiering. But that look on McGuire's face. No apology to the quiet soldier. The quiet man was right behind Bob. Was the bullet meant for *him*? And shortly before that, was it his imagination that had seen all points of the section's rifles pointed at him?

At this stage Bob stopped regarding close calls as lucky breaks. In war, he reasoned, you take what comes, even if it comes from your own side.

One may perhaps wonder why Bob did not seek out someone in whom to confide about his troubles with the clique, someone like Lieutenant John Petty, who had accompanied Bob on that healthy trek in the mountains near Darjeeling. Well, the Lieutenant received a promotion soon after the company arrived at Tiddim and Bob did not see him again. Not that he would have approached Lt Petty at all; Bob felt it was a problem he would have to deal with by himself. And on each suspicious occasion there seemed to be no proof of any bad action that he could pin on them. Neither did Bob even think of confiding in his only friend in the war, Bill Bell.

Bill Bell, an accountant by profession, was in charge of the regiment's transportation. He never saw action close up but was one of the many absolutely essential links in the whole war chain. On occasions when he and Bob met, such as during the drive from Imphal to Tiddim, and on some occasions when goods were delivered to Bob's section of the company they chatted about the weather, about home, about every day matters that friends talk about. Straight after the war, Bill went to Australia, where he settled. Bill was the only man in the war that Bob could call a friend.

At that time Bob had another inner turmoil, albeit a short one, when he shot his first Japanese soldier. His platoon investigated another hill. A group of Japanese soldiers on the summit evacuated the area quickly but a couple staged a short rearguard action by firing at Bob's men. Bob quickly lined up a man's chest in his sights and pulled the trigger. He saw the man collapse to the ground. In two more minutes the remaining Japanese had disappeared into the bush down the other side of the hill.

Bob went over to the body. The man was lying on his back with a bloody patch on his chest, one arm at his side and the other stretched out close to his rifle. The eyes stared at Bob in static accusation.

McGuire came up to look at the body.

"God they stink," he said.

Bob roused himself and organised the men to sweep downhill but they had no more contact with that enemy group.

That night when all the men were asleep in the tent at their base camp, Bob had a nightmare. He was back on the top of the hill, looking at the dead Japanese soldier. The figure rose up from the waist and stared at Bob with those accusing eyes. Then Bob's Anglican priest from his home town replaced the Japanese soldier. He was dressed in the usual cassock, surplus and robe, yet he had the same staring eyes as the Jap soldier.

"Thou shalt not kill," the priest intoned in a hollow voice.

Then, in the dream, Bob felt a heavy hand on his shoulder. He twisted his head to see his father behind him in his police uniform.

"Bob Robinson you are under arrest for murder," his father said.

Bob awoke and sat up with a gasp. He shivered as he looked at the rest of the men. They were all fast asleep.

PASSWORD

It was essential to be ready with the correct password when at war. The British and Indian infantry groups operating in similar areas made sure that they had a challenge word or phrase and a counter sign, word or phrase for the day. Normally, a new set of passwords would be used the next day. Passwords were used mainly for sentries and checkpoints behind your main lines, but small groups operating in countryside like that of Eastern India or Burma had also to be up to scratch with password use.

Bob told me that if your group or patrol was on its own for some time, even days, it was not always easy to do this, so British, Indian and Gurkha groups were in the habit of saying "Tikker-Jonnie" when encountering each other and that worked quite well. However, Bob told me about a group of Indian soldiers who settled in a treed area on top of a hill one night. The sentry or sentries saw an indistinct group of men walking by in the dark at the foot of their hill. The sentry called out "Ticker-Jonnie" and got the same call back. He saw the group below continue their walk at the foot of the hill then apparently away from it and fade into the dark.

The group at the foot of the hill were actually Japanese, who crept up the back of the hill and bayoneted all the Indian soldiers in their sleep.

RETREAT

Around this time, March 1944, the Japanese launch was in full swing. They pushed 100,000 men across the border, intent on driving the British, Indian and Gurkha troops from the Imphal Plain. Their advance in three prongs was very swift. The southern prong advanced on Tiddim, where Bob and his company were stationed. The second prong moved through the mountains and jungle towards the town of Imphal, and the third one moved further north, aimed at Kohima, at the northern end of the Imphal plain.

The British authorities decided that Tiddim was too thinly defended and ordered all their troops to retreat towards the city of Imphal. Another reason was to shorten the British supply line and thereby lengthen the Japanese supply line. The main British concentration was at Imphal, which was served by two airfields. Thus the 17th Indian division set out on its 100-mile trek northwards. The infantry walked, including their leader, Major-General Cowan, beside motorised and mule-laden transport.

They left Tiddim in flames, so as not to leave anything that could benefit the enemy. They took with them 4,000 mules and 2,000 vehicles. This is an important point because the Japanese leaders insisted on their men advancing as swiftly as possible. Where possible they used mules and even elephants to haul their artillery, but to ensure swift mobility each Japanese soldier carried little more than his weapon, ammunition and a three day rice ration in a sachet strung around his neck. They were ordered to live off the land and captured enemy food supplies.

Since the Japanese quick advance and the jungle terrain limited the number of vehicles they could bring along, they were ordered to use captured British vehicles for transport. For this reason they never destroyed abandoned enemy vehicles, something the British could benefit from at a later date.

Meanwhile, the 17th Division was moving *en masse* towards Imphal. Fast moving small clusters of Japanese troops harassed the rear and the sides of the 17th while some even established roadblocks ahead of the Division. The 17th gunners blasted these roadblocks away and infantry stormed through them to allow the wagons and vehicles to lumber through.

Closer to Imphal the Japanese managed to set up a large roadblock astride the Tiddim-Imphal road. To ensure that the 17th was not encircled, Major General Scoones, in command of the central front, ordered the 23rd Division to move south from the Ukhrul area and General Roberts, with the help of light tanks from the 7th Indian Cavalry, attacked and drove off the obstructing enemy.

Meanwhile, somewhere at the side of the middle section of the moving 17th, Bob and his platoon plodded on. At one point a British transport aeroplane flew quite low overhead and released a batch of supplies on parachutes. This was to be a saving and stimulating feature of the rest of the war. British Spitfire and Hurricane divisions from the Imphal airfields had by now greatly reduced the threat of Japanese attacks from the air, so transport planes were able to drop supplies to British and Indian troops throughout the Imphal campaign and indeed right up to the end of the war.

As Bob watched the welcome parachutes drift down, he felt the tiny sting of a mosquito on his neck. He slapped his sweaty neck, examined the little carcass and flicked it away. Damn mosquitoes! They were a constant nuisance. Then he noticed that one of the parachutes was drifting further away from the road than any of the others. In fact, it was caught in an eddy of wind that blew it over a long patch of trees.

"OK chaps," he called to his men, "Get to that one that drifted over those trees and haul it back here. There's a truck that is collecting all the bundles."

Before he had finished his words, the men were running down the slope to the trees. Bob walked after his men and observed other soldiers gathering canopies together and carrying the large bags and packages to the supply truck. When he got through the trees he saw his men pilfering various items from the large package that had split partly open. The men thrust packets of cigarettes, chocolate bars and other small items into their pockets and shirts. Anticipating Bob's arrival, some of the men grabbed hold of the chute and began gathering and folding it while the rest hauled the large package along a path through the trees and then up the slope to the supply truck.

Bob strode up the slope after his men. As they turned away from the truck, he stood in their way.

"OK men, I saw the pilfering."

The men looked at him as though they did not understand what he was saying.

"Since those items are distributed evenly among the troops you are depriving your own men, your own side in this war."

The men continued to stare back at him, not a guilty look among them.

The truck began to move off. A passing officer called out, "What are you lot loitering for? Get a move on!"

"Don't let me see that again," Bob said to his men.

His men turned, a couple with smiles on their faces, picked up their gear and continued the march like dedicated soldiers. On a previous occasion Bob had seen a couple of soldiers from another platoon pilfering small items from a supply package, so he concluded that this was a soldier thing, part of the make-up of these men, to be discouraged but not something he could take strong action against in the middle of a mass retreat.

A day later, Bob's group were still trudging on with the 17th towards Imphal. All were looking tired and sweating a lot. Bob particularly, was looking tired and was a little out of breath. He shook his head now and then as if to refocus his sight. Occasional shots were heard coming from either side of the long military caravan. Just then an officer approached Bob and pointed towards a spot to their right side.

"Sergeant!" he said, "Get your men into the jungle over there. Our flank guards seem to be having a bit of trouble there. Go see if you can help.

"Come on men!" Bob called, and trotted off, with his men following. They stopped at a canopy of trees and listened. They heard a few shots and set off in that direction through the trees. They came upon bush-type undergrowth and had to thread their way through it. They then came to a clearing where they paused. All was quiet. Then they heard the sound of boot-steps approaching them. They fell prone and kept completely silent.

Bob's heart was pounding as he peered towards the sound through a gap in the grass. Four khaki-clad figures filled his sight. They were fierce-looking Gurkha soldiers, armed to the teeth and moving parallel to the convoy.

"It's OK," he whispered to his men, "They're Gurkhas."

He gave a code whistle and call and he and his men stood up. The Gurkhas almost shot them, then relaxed.

"We were sent to help if you need us," Bob said to the warriors.

"No need," the lead Gurkha said, "We killed them. Six Japs."

He grinned and held out the palm of his hand. Six severed fingers lay on it. In his other hand he gripped a kukri, the vicious-looking curved short bladed knife that the Gurkhas make out of Bedford leaf springs. The blade bore traces of blood. The Gurkhas all smiled, raised a friendly hand and went on their way. Bob could only stare at the undergrowth through which they seemingly disappeared.

"Phew!" Fred breathed. "Am I glad they're on our side!"

The men half turned to go. Then they noticed that Bob continued to stare at the spot where the Gurkhas had exited. The branches and foliage there were swaying to and fro. He shook his head. The foliage was now still. He turned in the direction of the convoy.

"Let's get back," he muttered.

He led the way back through the undergrowth. He began to shiver, his legs wobbled, then he walked partly into a tree and fell to his knees.

McGuire gave a short laugh. "It's you who needs help from the Gurkhas, Sarge. Not vice-versa."

Fred got down beside Bob and examined his sweating face.

"You've got malaria."

"I'll be OK. Keep moving..."

He got half way up but collapsed. Now his shivering had increased and small moans escaped from his mouth. The others stood around him and looked down on him.

"Shhh!" Fred suddenly sounded.

They listened carefully. The sound of vegetation rustling! They all fell flat. Now they could hear footsteps accompanying the rustling.

Bob's shivering and groans had increased. Fred shoved a hand over Bob's mouth and two others sprawled over him to stop his shaking from disturbing the grass around him. Then they could hear what sounded like Japanese voices accompanying the trudging. They lay as quietly as possible until the sounds quietened, then finally were gone. Fred stood up stealthily, took a few steps in the direction of the passers-by then returned. He motioned for his men to go. Without a word, they all trod quietly away.

Bob shook his head to clear it. He got onto his elbows and peered at the foliage where his men had disappeared.

"What the...?"

He fumbled in the grass, feeling for his rifle. He found it and used it to struggle into a sitting position. He rested for a couple of minutes, then tried to lever himself up to a standing position. He was too weak. He stared at the surrounding vegetation. He wiped the sweat from his brow.

Then he heard a rustling in the vegetation ahead, getting closer. Japs? He managed to bring the rifle up into firing position in the right direction and he muttered through gritted teeth.

"I'll g-get a couple of you b-be-before you get me..."

The vegetation parted and Fred, Andy and young Greg appeared. For a second it looked as though Bob would fire.

"Hey Bob! It's us!" Fred blurted.

Bob lowered the rifle.

"Hell, you nearly shot us!" young Greg said.

The three of them got a hold of Bob, lifted him up and re-entered the undergrowth.

Shortly after that, the huge convoy lumbered into Imphal and deployed for the defence of the town and the area around it, including the two airfields. At a later date Bob wondered, since the men returned to fetch him, did that mean that all his doubts about them were wrong? But why did they at first leave him there?

Meanwhile, Bob was very sick with malaria in the Imphal hospital for a couple of days. It was decided to get as many of the sick and wounded as possible out of Imphal before it was surrounded by the Japanese forces. So Bob and all the sick and wounded were put into trucks and driven north along the 70 odd miles to Kohima, where they were again hospitalised. They had hardly settled in when they were again rushed onto the trucks and sent out of Kohima. Twelve hours after leaving, Japanese forces arrived and began surrounding Kohima and shelling it. That was on 3rd April 1944, so Bob escaped what was to become the deadliest and most important fight in this particular campaign.

KOHIMA

Although Bob was not involved in the Battle of Kohima , it is worth dwelling on it briefly, because it was the turning point of the campaign. Kohima, just north of the Imphal Plain, was the civil administrative centre, a supply depot with a hospital and a staging post. Most of its personnel were administrative.

The British were surprised at the speed at which the Japanese arrived near Kohima and so got as many of the admin staff out of Kohima as they could. If the Japanese were to capture Kohima, they would have moved westwards along the road to Diepenpur, an important railway centre, and the rest of India would have been open to them.

When the Japanese swarmed towards Kohima, they had to take various hills surrounding it and these hills were not given up lightly by the British. By the time the town was surrounded, the British side had about 2,000 British and Indian soldiers against about 13,000 Japanese soldiers. The British-held ground was reduced to a small area that was continually shelled, mortared and fired upon by the Japanese for seventeen days. At various points they were also subjected to several typical Japanese *Banzai* or mass charges – all of which ended in hundreds of dead Japanese soldiers littering the ground. In some places the opposing trenches were just 20 yards apart, so there was plenty of hand-to-hand fighting. The British had to rely on rifle fire, grenades, a little mortar capacity, Bren guns and some accurate artillery fire from two miles away. Amazingly accurate dropping of supplies by the RAF was vital, including the dropping of vehicle tyre tubes filled with water, vital because the garrison water supply had been cut off by the Japanese at an early stage. Only four parachute drops were lost out of 78!

The fiercest fighting took place where each side occupied one side of the District Commissioner's tennis court and blasted away at each other. The court was littered with dead and rotting corpses. The makeshift British field hospital was another desperate scene. The operating theatre was six feet deep and ten feet wide with a tarpaulin over it. Dr Colonel John Young worked at night in the flickering glow of hurricane lamps. Patients lying in the open and in slit trenches were in some cases wounded again or killed.

On 20th April 1944, Kohima was relieved but plenty of fighting went on to clear the dug-in Japs from surrounding hills and ridges. When the Kohima area battle was over the British and Indians had suffered 600 casualties, 200 of them dead. The Japanese had lost around 7,000 men.

All along the Kohima-Imphal road and westwards towards the Ukhrul area, the Japanese army was now in full retreat. Slim's plan was working – to draw the enemy to a pre-selected area and stand fast, denying the enemy food and stretching his lines of communication and supplies, finally to push him back.[3]

CLEARING THE IMPHAL PLAIN

"Clearing" is too soft a word, really. Once Kohima itself was relieved, British and Indian forces struggled for some time to eradicate fanatical Japanese troops entrenched in solid bunker positions in many areas around and south of Kohima. It was slow, bloody work, with significant losses on both sides. In his book *The Little Men*, Company Commander Ken W. Cooper describes the relentless, bloody struggle of his company in dreadful monsoon conditions against the stubborn Japanese east of Imphal.

---

[3] Most information on Kohima derived from *Not Ordinary Men* by John Colvin.

But let us return to Bob. At the start of the Kohima fight, Bob had been taken with the sick and wounded westwards along the road to Diepenpur where he spent a day lying on the ground in a tent hospital waiting for transport to take him to a proper hospital base. Apart from his fellow sick and wounded, the large tent was full of healthy-looking soldiers, lying or sitting on the groundsheets.

"What are all these men here for?" Bob asked a passing orderly.

"They're all VD patients," the orderly answered. "They come in from their units for a day, get treatment and then go back to their units." Bob had learnt something more about his fellow British soldiers.

From Diepenpur, Bob and many sick and wounded were taken to the British base at Silchar to recover in better medical surroundings. Silchar is situated 134 klms west of Imphal.

During its four month besiegement, Imphal was supplied entirely by air – an indication of the prowess of the RAF and some US airplanes. To reinforce besieged Imphal, the 5th Indian Division, complete with food, guns, mules and ammunition, was flown up from the Arakan and dropped in the heat of battle. By the end of the Imphal Plain battle, the air forces had flown 19,000 tons of supplies and 12,000 men into Kohima and Imphal and had flown out 13,000 casualties and 43,000 non-combatants. When Imphal was relieved, on 3rd July 1944, Bob re-joined his 17th Division, which had been in Imphal throughout the siege, and then moved south to take on the Japanese in the last phase of the Imphal Plain campaign.[4] The fighting was tough and in the fighting, British and Gurkha troops of 17th Division gained three VCs. But by now the 17th had been strengthened with the addition of motorised artillery, which blasted many of the Japanese well-built bunkers.

Bob remembers one group telling him that they came across a British prisoner who had been tied to a tree and used for bayonet practice. At other times prisoners were simply shot out of hand. There is just one incident on record, however, that was different. A few British soldiers were captured when their hill outside Kohima was overrun when the Kohima battle was in full swing. Their captors stripped them down to their underpants and returned them unharmed to the soldiers inside Kohima. When

---

[4] From *The Campaign In Burma*, Central Office of Information, British Govt.

Bob heard this he thought, that, deep down, there must be some good in them.[5]

J.J. Cherns, a lieutenant and platoon Commander with the 6th, the West African brigade, tells another interesting story. His platoon and a Japanese platoon were both dug in and firing at each other across the only water supply, a stream flowing between them. Both sides were beginning to suffer from thirst. In a lull in the fighting, a Jap soldier appeared holding a long stick with a white flag. He ran to the stream, filled a couple of canteens with water and ran back to his position. The Allies then did the same and filled a couple of their canteens with water. Each day, at the same time the procedure was repeated until the Jap platoon eventually retreated.[6]

Now the 17th had to head south and take the town of Potsangbam or "Pots and Pans" as the British soldiers called it, which the Japanese had used as headquarters for much of the Imphal campaign. There was stiff opposition to be overcome but the division was now strengthened with the addition of Sherman tanks to blast the enemy bunkers. Nevertheless Bob remembers feeling relieved that he was short, because on a couple of occasions bullets whizzed over his head. He saw one tall soldier get shot in the head and killed instantly.

One incident Bob remembers at this time, about half way through May 1944, was when a young officer joined his group in an attack on a Japanese position. They were being shelled by enemy artillery. Bob, like the other soldiers, had become attuned to the sound of an incoming shell. Usually you heard the distant thump of the big gun firing, then you heard the whine and then you heard the scream – and that's when you dropped down flat on the ground. When one was heard coming close, Bob threw himself to the ground but the young officer in front of Bob was slow to react. He landed beside Bob, unhurt. They looked at each other. The officer looked sheepish.

The group got to its feet and advanced closer to the town. When they approached a wall of soil obscuring their view of the town, the young officer climbed quickly up and stood on the top, just as the scream of a second shell approached. Bob and his men flattened themselves on the ground. There was an explosion on the other side of the wall. The young

---

[5] From *Forgotten Voices from Burma* by Julian Thompson.
[6] Ibid.

officer landed beside Bob again, this time dead from the shrapnel that had struck him.

Several young officers died in incidents like that. Bob says it was just not done for a soldier to give an officer advice unasked. The officers themselves did not wish to show that they were not brave, nor did they want to seem ignorant in front of their troops. Thus the hierarchy/class system in the army had some unfortunate consequences.

Bob remembers another officer incident. It concerned a Sergeant Major whose name Bob cannot remember but whose conduct he admired, who never swore and seemed never to lose his temper in his daily dealings in the army. He was fairly close to Bob's section when an enemy canon opened up on their position. Everyone in the vicinity dived for cover, including the officer, who took refuge behind a row of sandbags. A piece of shrapnel went clean through the sandbag and killed the officer. The sandbags were all filled with soil, not sand. Sand will stop a bullet or a small piece of shrapnel, but soil will not. Bob never heard whether anyone looked into the matter.

It was while fighting near Potsangbam that Bob had another extraordinary escape. He was advancing with his men towards a bund that was about five feet high. The men were all moving in crouched positions. They believed there were Japanese in the area but had not yet come across them. The bund had big gaps in it where shell fire or other activity had levelled parts of it. When the men moved through the gaps they were confronted by a second bund, undamaged and also about five feet high stretching parallel to the first one. The men settled on their knees or sat down between the two bunds for a brief respite.

All was very quiet so Bob decided that as sergeant he should look over the top of the second bund to ascertain if all was clear. As he lifted his head above the level of the bund all he could see was a foliage hedge some fifteen yards away. There was a sudden rattle of machine gun fire through the hedge and he could almost feel the swish the bullets around his head and his bush hat was swept off. He fell flat on the ground. A couple of his men threw grenades in the direction of the source of machine gun fire. After the explosions they stood up and fired into the hedge, then scrambled over the bund and advanced to find they had killed the Japanese machine gun crew.

A shaken Bob stood up and saw that the section of first bund behind his head had an almost neat semi-circle of bullet holes around the shape of his head. He concluded that the rattling of the machine gun firing caused the barrel to move in a slight circle as he had observed in previous observations of the firing of British static machine-guns. The small circle of flying bullets widened just enough as they approached Bob's head to whiz past and around it. It was a miracle, he concluded.

The British took the town of Potsangbam in the end. The area was littered with dead Japanese. The vast majority of Japanese soldiers were trained to see surrender as cowardice so they fought to the death. Knowing this, the British and allies generally gave no quarter. Any Japanese with a weapon was shot instantly. Lieutenant Mahesh Sharma of the 7th Independent Fields Company, Bengal sappers and miners, is quoted as saying, "I saw a Japanese officer with part of his arm missing and maggots crawling over him, still fighting."[7]

DISEASE AND HYGENE

One cannot get a full picture of the British campaign in this region without taking a glimpse at the medical situation. At this time the numbers of soldiers on the Imphal Plain contracting typhus from tick bites was growing and it was found that many were dying when being flown back to the hospital at Camilla. Because of this, and a shortage of male orderlies, it was decided that a certain number of nurses would be flown to medical casualty stations quite near the front, to treat the patients until they got over the worst of the disease. In the "WW2 People's War" Charlie Raull reports the words of his mother, Nurse Kitty Calcutt, when she was flown and driven by jeep to "Mile 64", a medical casualty station 64 miles from Imphal.

> *"All around us was jungle. One large tent held diagnosed typhus patients. Almost immediately a convoy of men arrived and had to be given 'beds'. These were stretchers balanced on four forked sticks – no number, no diagnosis. The doctor said first take the T.P.R. (temperature, pulse, respiration) then give the lot malaria treatment."* [8]

These nurses played an important part in the overall British system of providing medical care for its fighters.

---

[7] From *Forgotten Voices from Burma* by Julian Thompson Page.
[8] Charlie Raull in the WW2 People's War Forum (bbc.co.uk/ww2peopleswar)

120 sick servicemen were evacuated for every one wounded man in this theatre of the war. As the war progressed, the arrival of forward medical teams, the evacuation of the sick and wounded by light aircraft, sometimes from short airstrips cut out of jungle, and the innovation of jeep ambulances served to diminish the ravages of disease and increase the chances of recovery for the many sick and wounded.

General Slim threatened to sack any regimental officer who failed to see that his troops took their daily dose of *mepacrine* anti-malarial medicine. He often checked up on officers to see that they were making their men adhere to basic health issues such as washing hands regularly. Ken Cooper explains how when on a mission his men settled for a day or more beside a river or a stream they would use the upper part beside their camp for washing themselves, the middle part for the washing of utensils, pans and equipment and the lower part for basic personal ablutions. The latter procedure ensured that evidence of their presence would be washed away.

It is interesting to note that contributor "Russ" tells us in the *War Relics Forum*[9] on the Internet that his grandfather passed down to him a rusty tin shaving container in which was a three-part old safety razor. Amazingly, the grandfather had managed to keep this throughout his stay in a Japanese prison camp in Burma – such was his determination to keep himself as clean as he could.

Bob also used an old three-part safety razor with a Gillette blade for most of his time in India and Burma. He regarded shaving as regularly as possible as a necessary part of his self-cleanliness. Before he left England he made himself a mirror for use while in the East. He found a suitable mirror 6 inches long by 3 inches wide. Then he fashioned a leather backing for it slightly bigger than the mirror itself then folded the thin but strong leather over the edges of the mirror and secured them together at the corners with leather washers. Just below the top edge of the leather he made a small hole so that the shaving mirror could be nailed to a tree. Bob also kept a small shaving brush with a boxwood handle. By lathering a little soapy water he was able to shave. After the war Bob still had the little shaving brush whose bristles were very worn down.

Each soldier had two backpacks. He always took with him the bigger one, containing all he would need while on the move. He had to leave

---

[9] War Relics Forum (www.warrelics.eu/forum/)

behind the smaller one containing less essential items such as shaving gear. The smaller bags were taken by truck and delivered to the men periodically when they were stationed in an area for a few days. Quite late in the war, Bob and his men were waiting for the arrival of their small packs at a village somewhere near Pegu, on the road to Rangoon. The packs did not arrive. They learnt later that a group of Punjabi men had been transporting the packs but that, when nearing their destination, they had taken what they wanted from the packs and discarded them. The packs were later found but Bob's shaving mirror was no longer in his pack.

BACK TO TIDDIM

The 17th now moved on southwards towards its old positions outside Tiddim. Bob remembers one occasion when his platoon crept softly up a hill. They had reason to believe that a group of Japanese were on the top. The Japanese were not expecting trouble and the platoon were able to creep on their bellies quite close to them. The nearest man to them was a sentry who was facing the wrong way. Fred threw a grenade to start the onslaught. The explosion sliced off the top of the sentry's head. A portion of brain matter landed on the ground right in front of Bob's head. He recoiled on his haunches while the rest of the platoon opened up on the Japanese and charged at them. A soldier tossed two grenades into a bunker and in little time the summit was full of dead Japanese. When there were no more signs of life from the bunker, Bob and his men continued down the other side and went to finish off the survivors among the shrubbery.

As the Japanese were pushed further back, Bob was able to visit Fort White and the 8,800ft Kennedy Peak, which had been his group's haunts at the beginning of Bob's fighting stint. In his book *From Defeat to Victory*, General Slim mentions that Bob's 9th Brigade was the leading brigade in this part of the campaign and how one of its battalions went round Kennedy Peak to cut off the Japanese retreat towards the Burma border.

> *"After frantic and costly efforts to break through, they (the Japanese forces) broke up into small parties, and, abandoning everything except their small arms, took to the surrounding jungle."*[10]

---

[10] *From Defeat Into Victory* by Field Marshal Sir William Slim, p.263, Cassell & Co Ltd, London, Second Edition, March 1956.

Tiddim was retaken by the British on 17th October 1944 and by 9th November 1944 Kennedy Peak and Fort White were occupied. By the 14th November the British and allies were occupying Kalewa on the Chindwin river. The stage was set to carry the war back into Burma.

By December 1944 victorious flags flew all over the Imphal Plain. Fifty thousand Japanese soldiers lay dead, along with 17,000 mules, bullocks and pack ponies. The 14th Army had suffered 17,000 casualties but its spirits soared. "Imphal" means "flower on lofty heights" – its elevated natural beauty was restored.

At this point Bob and his men were given a two-week break from war and sent to Gulmarg, a popular winter resort at 8,500ft in Nepal. Bob and his men enjoyed a return to fresh mountain air.

Bob and Bill Bell at Gulmarg.

This was another time to unwind, to relax. It was not really a time to ponder on his fighting experiences or even on the vexation of living with the clique. He had an eye for nature, appreciated scenery and took this time to enjoy the mountains again.

IN PURSUIT

The big push back into Burma had begun but movement among the high mountains and jungle terrain was difficult, to say the least, in the border regions. Most of the 'roads' were just tracks. They had first to be widened.

Bob was very impressed by the Indian sappers and labourers. Armed only with a mattock, each man would strike at the inner wall of the track/road until he had a pile of loose soil and gravel. He would pick this up with the flat side of the mattock, carry it over to the sheer side of the road, drop and level it to widen the road. They worked like this, day after day.

Indian sappers at work on a road (from Campaign in Burma, Central Office of Information, London 1946).

Many of the mountain tracks and roads were very steep and windy and some had precipitous sides to them. While going along one such downhill road, Bob's Indian driver was a bit slow in turning the wheel at a corner. The truck began to slide. When the driver slammed on the brakes, the vehicle kept on sliding. With a yell the driver baled out of his side of the truck, as did Bob's platoon. Bob had no option but to do the same and landed just feet away from the edge. The truck came to rest with its front wheels balancing on the very edge of a precipice. As everyone watched with bated breath, the truck made creaking noises but then settled in that awkward position.

Bob looked at his men, who were all staring at the truck and making noises of relief. There was no sign of the driver.

"Any ideas what to do?" Bob said.

The men were silent. Bob walked over to a couple of solid but flat rocks by the inner side of the road. He took hold of one and lifted it.

"Fred, give me a hand here," he said.

Fred came over and lifted the other rock. They carried them to the truck and each inserted his rock under the truck in front of the rear tyres. Bob faced the men again.

"Any of you driven a truck before?" he asked.

The men looked at each other but remained perfectly quiet.

"Who will volunteer to reverse it?"

Silence.

Bob heaved a sigh and climbed carefully into the truck on the driver's side. He had never driven a truck before. He made sure the gears were in neutral. He waited, then breathed evenly. He started the engine. Then he put the gear into reverse and pushed down on the accelerator. The engine roared, the vehicle appeared to move back a little, the tires squealed and it went forward to its original position and wobbled. Bob closed his eyes, put the gear into neutral and took his foot off the accelerator. He waited a full minute, then tried again. This time the rear wheels caught and the truck moved mercifully backwards. Bob straightened the truck on the road, then moved back to the passenger seat and shouted out of the side window.

"All aboard men!"

The Indian driver reappeared and took up his position in the driver's seat.

"Very good Sir, very good Sir," he said.

The men clambered onto the back of the open truck. The truck moved off. Bob put a hand on his sweaty forehead.

The truck continued for a few minutes then the driver moved the vehicle slowly around another blind bend. When the road straightened out again it widened. They saw a solitary thin figure sitting on a rock on the inner side of the road. He looked terrified.

"He a driver," Bob's driver said.

Their truck stopped, Bob got out and went up to the man.

"What's the matter?"

The driver simply pointed to a section of the road edge. Bob walked over to the spot and saw tyre skid marks in the soil, ending at the edge. He looked over the edge. A sheer drop of about a hundred feet ended on a large flat ledge where a crushed, up-ended military truck lay. The distorted bodies of soldiers were scattered on the ledge and half under the truck. Bob's men jumped off their truck and came over to view the carnage. They whistled and gasped in their amazement.

Just then another truck came lumbering around the corner and pulled up behind Bob's truck. The door opened and a major got out and walked up to Bob. Bob saluted the Major.

"What's the hold-up Sergeant?"

Bob just looked down at the skid marks. The Major also looked at the skid marks then peered over the edge. His face went white.

"The driver down there too?"

Bob shook his head.

"No Sir," he said.

"Where is he?" the Major asked.

They all turned as the thin driver appeared and came forward with a trembling hand held up in acknowledgement.

The Major looked at the driver, drew his revolver and shot him in the head. Blam!

Everyone else jerked a step backwards. The shot echoed in the surrounding mountains.

The major walked back to his truck, got in and drove off.

Bob's men were very silent for a long time as their truck made its way on down the hill. As Bob told me, only a senior officer could make and carry out an instant decision like that.

THE KABAW VALLEY

"We had entered a place of evil enchantment"
(from *Nemesis* by Max Hastings)

At the foot of the Tamu Pass and the long, winding roads on the sides of mountains, Bob's convoy now entered the territory of Burma. They moved southwards along the long Kabaw Valley, regarded as one of the most pestilence-ridden valleys in the world. It is often called Death Valley. In Bob's time it consisted of a track with not many wide parts, meandering through a seemingly endless swamp. The water looked pitch black because of the black soil beneath it and most of the vegetation consisted of swamp trees with big bundles of roots rising high above the water line. One heard the constant whine and screech of every kind of insect, especially mosquitoes. From time to time a snake slithered from the water and across the track.

Much earlier in the war, hundreds of civilian men, women, children and soldiers had fled through the valley to escape from the advancing Japanese army and to reach India. Bob tried to imagine the civilians, clad in normal shoes and clothes struggling along this God-forsaken route. Few survived. Many died from the deadly scrub typhus which infected the place.

The time had come for the Japanese soldiers to have their turn to run this terrible gauntlet. The track was wider and firmer now. An East African regiment had gone before Bob's group to harass the retreating Japanese from the rear and to improve the road as they went. The Japanese soldiers had been deserted by many of their leaders, their supply lines, always minimal, were now non-existent and they were suffering from malnutrition, diseases and exhaustion. Furthermore, they had the RAF to contend with. RAF pilot Merton Naydler, with a Hurricane squadron, bombed and strafed the Japanese all the way along the Kawbaw Valley. He writes:

> *"Our aggressiveness and sense of destruction increased day by day, as our bombing became increasingly accurate."*[1]

When the Japanese were pushed out of their base at Tamu, at the northern most tip of the Kawbaw Valley, bulldozers flattened and cleared a strip big enough for Dakotas, which transported the squadron's technical and personal equipment and 200 odd ground staff. The strip was also used by Auster ambulance aircraft, which flew out the wounded. Bulldozers were an important part of the 14th Army's equipment. Towards the end of January 1945, Dakotas airlifted everything down to Kanu, much further down the Kabaw Valley, and set up base beside two new strips cleared by the bulldozers so the RAF fighters and ambulance planes could carry on with their work closer to the front. At Imphal, the RAF coined the phrase: "The impossible we do at once – miracles take a little longer."

---

[1] *Young Man You'll Never Die* by Merton Naydler, p.186, Isis large print Reminiscence Series.

Bob's convoy moved down this road near the Burma border. (from Campaign in Burma, Central office of Information, London 1946).

Back to the ground fighting – from his truck, moving along the Kabaw valley, Bob saw half bodies/half skeletons in torn Japanese uniforms sprawled at the side of the road. Some bodies still in one piece were partly covered in bloodied bandages. The truck drew up alongside a Jap jeep with three skeleton occupants still sitting in the seats. They'd been eaten clean by white ants.

Soldier J.J. Cherns, in his *Private Papers*[12] reported a similar spectacle. When his group emerged from the Kabaw Valley and went into the deserted village of Maulaik they found several skeletons sitting around a table in a hut.

At one point in the Kabaw Valley, Bob got out of his truck and took a closer look at some of the corpses. He had to hold his nose because of the stench. Some lay as though asleep, still in their stocking'd feet. They carried only a mess tin, steel helmet and a rifle. In one spot several men lay curled close together as though seeking warmth from each other as the coldness of death crept over them. Some, probably half mad from hunger and explosions, had killed themselves with their own grenades. Max Hastings[13] reports how two prisoners were revived with hot tea. They put their heads in their hands and wept and cried like children. It was a disgrace for them to be alive.

Bob stooped beside a mere boy and saw his diary lying beneath his bayonet. He picked up the diary and turned a few pages. Some miniature watercolour paintings were interspersed with neat Japanese script smudged by rust from the bayonet. Here was budding talent, Bob mused to himself, an artist or writer whose life was cut short by war. Just a boy.

Then Bob thought of the British soldier tied to a tree and used for bayonet practice. He placed the diary where he had found it and walked back to the truck. Beside the truck young Greg was looking at a couple of corpses.

"What's in the little bag tied with string around their necks?" he asked Bob.

"Three days' supply of rice," Bob answered. "They're expected to feed themselves from the wild or from captured British supplies."

"Why didn't these eat their rice rations?"

"Too starved, weak or sick to cook it or eat it."

"Let's get the hell out of this stinking place!" McGuire shouted from the truck.

As much as these sights horrified Bob, he was more horrified by the thought of the civilians – men, women and children – who came along this dreadful route, attempting to escape to India from the victorious Japanese army at the start of the war. He pictured them in his mind – wearing

---

[12] Private Papers of J.J. Cherns 03/23/1 (www.iwm.org.uk).
[13] Max Hastings. *Nemesis.*

civilian clothes and shoes, a child dying of malaria in her fathers' arms, people starving, women falling by the wayside from sheer exhaustion.

TO CROSS A RIVER

When Bob's regiment emerged from the Kabaw Valley, one of the first obstacles they had to face was getting across the Myittha River, a tributary of the Chindwin River. It was not a very big river but boats, pontoons and rafts had to be used to get men, vehicles and equipment across, and there was a shortage of these. Bob's men managed to get across by squeezing onto various pontoons and rafts but Bob stayed on the departure shore until all his men were across. Beside him a group of Gurkhas started building a boat from bamboo and wood. Bob ignored them and set about making his own means of crossing.

He spread his large waterproof gas cape, like a large ground sheet, flat on the ground beside the water. Then he placed two straight, thick bamboo poles, plugged at each end, in the middle across the cape, about two and a half feet apart. Then he put his kitbag and other items firmly between the two poles, then folded the ends of the cape over the top of the bundle and, using rope, laced the ends of the cape together through the buttonholes. He then pushed the bundle onto the water, placed his rifle on the top and waded into the water until he had to swim, pushing the bundle before him.

He made three trips like that, taking light equipment across. He had finished his third crossing before the Gurkhas had completed their bamboo boat.

ACROSS THE BURMA PLAINS

Some of the army divisions moved directly east and crossed the Chindwin River, which had been the last major hurdle for the men who retreated from the Japanese in 1941. Now the re-crossing of the river heralded the army's unstoppable resurgence. The 17th Division, however, moved with other divisions out of the Kabaw Valley, south of the Chindwin's curve towards the Irrawaddy River and started the "dash" across the Burma plain.

The first thing Bob's section came across was a long line of mules packed with large hessian bags moving in the opposite direction. Burmese villagers walked beside them. A major in the vehicle in front of Bob's truck stepped out with an interpreter and a soldier armed with a Tommy gun and approached the lead villager. Bob also got out of his truck and went forward. The interpreter did his work as the major and the villager spoke in turn.

"Who is in charge of these mules?"

"Me Sahib. I am the village headman."

"What are the mules carrying and where are you taking them?"

"It is all rice. The Japanese gave us money to take it to them in the mountains. They said they will kill us if we do not."

"Well then, my man, you have nothing to worry about. Turn your mules around and take the rice back to your homes."

"Thank you, thank you Sahib."

The village head beamed and held up his hands in supplication then ran back, shouting the good news to his men who were all soon jabbering and turning their mules around.

General William Slim had cleverly sent the detachments that crossed the Chindwin River towards the Irrawaddy River north of Mandalay to make the Japanese troops east of the Irrawaddy believe that the main British attack would cross the river and attack Mandalay from the north. The plan worked because most of the Japanese detachments moved in that direction. Meanwhile the 17th Division, now motorised and with tank support, was racing across the Burma plain to the south of Mandalay and heading for Meiktila, the huge Japanese communications and supply centre.

By February 1945 the 17th were crossing the Irrawaddy. Vehicles were taken across on pontoons. Other boats and pontoons full of troops were slowly putt-putting across the wide river, pushed by little "seagull" outboard motors. More complex transport machinery was not shipped or flown in to India or Burma because the war in Europe took precedence.

ACROSS THE IRRAWADDY

Soon after crossing the Irrawaddy, Bob remembers an incident when his truck came across the bodies of four dead Japanese soldiers which Burmese peasants were busy stripping of all clothing and weapons, leaving them clad only in loin-cloths. This was to become a common sight during the rest of the war. In the early part of the war the Japanese had told the local population that they were freeing them from British imperialism but the locals soon learnt that their new overlords were far worse, hence many groups of locals harassed the Japanese during their retreat.

As Bob and his men, along with other infantry units, advanced towards Meiktila, they took part in a lot of action. On one occasion when they were advancing towards a village in extended order, as they approached a long, low bank shots were fired at them. They all fell flat. The bank was a bunker. Shots were whizzing all around them but the men were able to keep low or find refuge behind tree stumps or rocks. They then heard shouts from behind them telling them to stay low because their own artillery was about to open fire.

Bob blocked his ears as the din and boom of the artillery opened up for a good fifteen minutes. The bunkers were enveloped in explosions with earth and wood spurting high into the air. The artillery ceased fire and then several tanks manned by Indian soldiers clattered their way between the groups of infantry and fired their shells into the bunkers at point-blank range. Several of the tanks then moved right over the ruined bunkers, crushing them further. The infantry stood up and followed the tanks. Now and then a Jap would rise from the rubble and flee but would immediately be shot down. Some badly wounded Japs were found leaning half out of holes and were dispatched with single shots.

As Bob made his way over a mangled part of a bunker he heard a cry. He stopped and listened. Again he heard the cry. He knelt down and saw that the cries were coming from a small hole in a smashed concrete part of a bunker. He listened for a minute to the pathetic, pleading cries. He took out a grenade, pulled out the pin, dropped the grenade down the hole and walked on. There was a muffled explosion behind him.

As Bob told me, "I thought it was better to end his suffering."

As Bob's platoon, amidst other infantry platoons, got nearer to Meiktila, they approached a Japanese hospital, made of bamboo with wooden sides and thick straw roofing. Rifle barrels protruded from the open windows and shots were fired at the advancing troops. The British fell flat. The patients had been armed and instructed to fight to the end. As Bob and his men lay prone, McGuire fixed his bayonet to his rifle.

"Let's go stick them like pigs," he said. "That's what they did to one of our field hospitals."

Indeed, in the southern area of the war, on the Arakan Peninsular on the coast, an Allied field hospital had been overrun by Japanese soldiers who rampaged through it, bayoneting and shooting everyone, including the doctors.

"No," was Bob's answer.

McGuire and a couple of the men looked in annoyance at Bob. Bullets fired from the hospital still whizzed uncomfortably overhead.

"We will wait for orders," Bob concluded.

No sooner had he said it, than a group of infantry began firing tracer bullets at the hospital. Most soldiers were issued with a few tracer bullets among their normal quota, usually as a way of indicating an enemy position at night to bigger guns. Bob and his men watched as the thatched roof of the hospital caught fire, then spread to the walls and then engulfed the whole building in a conflagration as the screams of the Japanese patients filled the air.

Half an hour later the British soldiers walked alongside the collapsed blackened walls and surveyed the burnt corpses lying on smouldering cots or on the floor. One blackened figure still crouched and grasped his gun as it rested on the windowsill. A few of the patients had managed to run outside but had collapsed with horrific burns to most of their bodies. Two of them were still screaming in agony. Single shots to the head ended their misery. The 17th Division went on to secure the airfields on the outskirts of Meiktila.

Private Peter Hazelhurst of 9th Battalion B Company, reported that it was difficult to hold onto the airfield.[14] The enemy managed to shell it for some time and Japanese snipers tied themselves onto branches of trees on the side of the airstrips and sniped at the British occupying the airfield. It went on for eight days until soldiers solved the problem by walking about five yards apart from each other, spraying the trees with Tommy gun and Bren gun fire.

An interesting example of how the RAF worked with the army at this time is provided by Pilot Merton Nydler:[15]

> "At Pakokku, 58 miles west of Meiktila, the Japanese were holding out against all the army's efforts to dislodge them. With a five hundred

---

[14] Private Peter Hazelhurst in *Forgotten Voices of Burma* by Julian Thompson.
[15] From *Young Man You'll Never Die* by Ralf Naydler.

pound bomb under each wing we repeatedly bombed and strafed them and that did the job."

It took four days (March 1st to March 4th 1945) of heavy fighting to capture Meiktila. Gurkha and British troops and Indian-driven tanks fought their way from bunker to bunker and from street to street. Almost all the Japanese fought to the death. As was the case throughout this advance the RAF parachuted supplies to the British side and landed wherever and whenever they could to unload more supplies and to evacuate the sick and wounded.

Men of 17th Division charging towards Meiktila (from magazine "On to Rangoon" Indian War Department 1946).

It was not easy to hold onto Meiktila. Japanese soldiers were moved from other areas and were able to surround the 17th Division in Meiktila. Major Cowan had a good way of dealing with this situation. He kept quite a small number of men, such as Bob's platoon, in defensive positions, and sent out columns in different directions to strike at Japanese communications and groups of enemy soldiers. Writer George M. Fraser's platoon was with one of these columns and was heavily engaged in the fighting. In this way

Major Cowan prevented a big build-up of the enemy in one place to attack in force.

Dead Japanese soldiers outside Meiktila (from Magazine "On to Rangoon" Indian War Department 1946).

MAGGOTS

When the fighting in Meiktila was over, Bob's platoon and many other infantrymen were sitting at the side of a road, smoking and chatting. Bob stood on the outskirts and watched the men of his platoon. They were joking with each other and talking about drinking and their escapades with women. 'This is what they live for,' he thought, 'the time between the fighting when they drink together, joke together, discuss what they did during their last leave. Then they go to confession on Friday to salve their conscience and then it's back to their day-to-day life.' In action they were not bad soldiers but the war and what they were doing in it and why they were doing it seemed to be of little importance to them.

Bob was always restless at a time like this. He strolled a short way along the street, looking at the empty, half-demolished buildings. Although its walls bore the familiar bullet scars, one of the buildings was completely intact. Keeping his gun handy, he entered the doorway. On the ground floor he looked carefully into each room. Some contained empty, dusty desks and chairs, some smashed. One room showed patches of dried blood on the floor. He came to a stairway and walked carefully up to the second floor. As he entered the corridor, he paused and readied his rifle at chest level. A pair of khaki clad legs with the usual Japanese stocking'd calf area protruded into the corridor through a doorway. The legs moved slightly. Then they were still. Then they trembled just a little. Bob trod softly towards the legs, then swung into the doorway with rifle at the ready. A massive stink invaded his nostrils and he saw that from the man's neck down to his thighs millions of maggots squirmed and jostled as they feasted. Bob stumbled backwards into the corridor, turned and vomited on the floor, then strode away with hunched shoulders. That was the last time he investigated a building on his own.

A happier incident in the same war involving maggots was when a very badly injured Royal Indian Air Force pilot, Battacharjen, was pulled from his shot-down airplane and left in a coma in a shack to die. A doctor found him some days later, covered in maggots. He was hospitalised and brought back to good health. The doctor said that the maggots helped heal his injuries by eating away the infection and toxins from the wounds.[16]

After the fall of Meiktila, British and Indian forces moved northwards from Meiktila to attack Mandalay, the second most important city in Burma. The troops who had crossed the Irrawaddy further north moved southwards to attack Mandalay from the north while more troops crossed the Irrawaddy and attacked from the southeast. The city was heavily defended and fierce fighting took place. Merton Naydler's Hurricane

---

[16] From Bharat Rakshak's Indian Air Force website, *Flying Operations on the Burma Front.*

squadron were also heavily engaged in this fighting. The 17th Division did not take part in this battle but anyone wishing to read about it should read Field Marshal Sir William Slim's book *Defeat Into Victory*.

ANOTHER SNAKE ENCOUNTER

By the end of March 1945, Mandalay had been recaptured. Although Bob's 17th Division did not take part in the fighting at Mandalay, it carried out numerous patrolling and mopping-up operations in the surrounding area. While on one of these patrols, three platoons, including Bob's, knowing that there were Japanese not far away, dug in on one side of a small river in preparation for the night.

Bob dug his trench close to the river, deep enough for him to stand in it and shoot comfortably over the lip and across the river if necessary. He also made sure to provide a firm step half way up the side to ensure easy entry and exit.

He had just finished perfecting his trench when he heard a commotion in a neighbouring bushy area. He stood up on the step and, in the next instant, two large Burmese pythons came slithering out of the bush to-wards him. One veered to one side and slid straight into the river. The other slithered beside a very startled Bob and fell into his trench. There Bob stood on the step, frozen in fright, eyes glued to the unwelcome visitor now thrashing about at the bottom of his trench.

At that point, three soldiers burst through the bush. They had been chasing the pythons. The snakes must have been mating at the time because that is about the only time that Burmese pythons do not stay alone. The python reared up its ugly head and gaped and gulped with its big mouth close to Bob's face. Before Bob could react, one of the soldiers snatched up Bob's entrenching spade that was lying on the edge of the trench and swung a hefty blow down at the python. The sharp edge of the spade cleaved the python in two. Incredibly, the head on the part standing up near Bob continued to gape and gulp for half a minute before collaps-ing.

The soldier apologized for disturbing Bob's peace, retrieved the two parts of the snake and made off with it. Perhaps he wanted to try to remove the snake's skin, Bob thought. After that, Bob was as vigilant of nature's dangers as he was of those of the war.

ON THE ROAD TO RANGOON

It was during that time that Bob recalls an incident concerning a young officer. Bob told me that he admired the young officers who from time to time joined the platoon; they were brave and keen but inexperienced. One day the platoon was moving cautiously through dry summer paddy fields. Each field was separated by a low mud wall called a *bund*. It was not an uncommon sight to see a cobra emerge from a hole in a bund and slither along before sliding into another hole, so the men were wary of cobras as well as of the enemy. They came to a bund that was higher than the rest, higher than the tallest of the men. The men took a breather at this point and took sips from their water bottles.

A young officer who had been walking beside Bob turned and said, "Well, we've had a quiet day so far, haven't we?"

Bob smiled at the young officer and nodded in agreement.

"I think I'll just take a look around," the young officer said, and walked towards the bund. When he got to the base he got on all fours and started to climb up it.

"Wait Sir! Don't!" Bob called out, but the officer did not hear the warning, got to the top of the bund and stood up. Immediately a shot rang out and a bullet whizzed past his head, giving his helmet the slightest nick. The young man jumped down from the bund, fell to his knees, then sprang up and, with a terrified look in his eyes, ran as fast as he could in sheer panic.

Bob dropped his gun, stepped into his way, grabbed him around the chest, flattened his own head against the taller young officer's chest so as to avoid being punched, then held on as strongly as he could and muttered, "It's all right Sir. It's OK. Calm down Sir."

As the man's shivering began to ease and he began to breathe evenly, Bob let him go. The officer regained his composure and walked away. His platoon were already moving along the bund, looking for lower parts of it through which to advance, so Bob did not think his men saw the officer's panic. Bob never saw or heard from that officer again.

ELEPHANTS

Hannibal used elephants as heavy cavalry or even the equivalent of tanks in his wars against Rome. Ancient India and other Eastern countries also used them against their enemies. In Burma during World War II both sides made use of elephants for transporting supplies. Bob remembers that it was around this time that he came across elephants used in this way.

While his and other platoons were patrolling and mopping up they came across three adult elephants and a young one being escorted by Burmese coolies and a couple of Burmese soldiers that were on the Japanese side. On the back of each adult elephant was a large bulging tarpaulin secured with ropes stretching under its belly.

Upon being challenged by a British officer, the two Burmese soldiers threw down their rifles and raised their hands in surrender. The officer sent a few of his men to help the coolies undo the ropes and offload the cargo, which turned out to be an assortment of Japanese guns and boxes of ammunition. The Burmese soldiers were supposed to take the cargo to Japanese soldiers but quickly agreed to hand everything over to the British. The elephants were then used, together with their handlers, to carry supplies for the British.

Here's another elephant occurrence: after serving as an infantry officer in the First World War, James Howard Williams settled in Burma, went into the Teak business and became the boss of the elephant teams. When the Japanese swept across Burma he took his family into India on the back of an elephant through the Kabaw Valley. He then returned to Burma, rounded up as many elephants as he could and set to work with his *mahouts* or *uzies* – hauling logs of wood for the building of bridges and culverts and to take supplies to isolated Allied troops. They even worked as 'sappers", pounding wooden stakes into the ground with tusks or feet. James joined the staff of the British 14th Army as Elephant Adviser and was praised for his invaluable service by Field Marshal Sir William Slim.[17]

Another remarkable use of elephants in this war was made in June 1942 when a 53-year old Englishman named Gyles Mackrel, who worked on a tea plantation in Assam, India, took a group of mahouts and elephants on a 100-mile trek to the Dapha River, where he rescued 200 refugees who were fleeing from the advancing Japanese army, by transporting them across the swollen river on the backs of the elephants. The event has been dubbed *The Far Eastern Dunkirk*. It is rather heartening to see the elephant graduating from weapon to transporter to rescuer.[18]

---

[17] Source: Mail Online 1st November www.dailymail.co.uk.
[18] Source BBC online www.bbc.co.uk/news/

DOGS AND VULTURES

While stationed at a village during this stage of the war, an abundance of feral dogs (known as *pariah* dogs) in the area became a real nuisance. One day a group of them managed to get into a *basha* stocked with rations. Virtually every can of food was flattened and punctured with teeth marks. The adjutant was furious.

"Get rid of those damn dogs, sergeant!" he ordered Bob. He walked away without saying how Bob should go about it.

Bob went to the quartermaster's stores and chose a sniper rifle – a smarter, sleeker version of the .303 Lee Enfield that the soldiers carried. Bob removed the telescopic sights. He scouted around the areas outside the village to ascertain the places that the dogs frequented. He chose one area and early one morning crawled under a hedge, from which he had a clear view of the creatures and began picking them off. When one area was depleted of dogs, he moved to another. In three days he killed 90 pariah dogs.

On the second evening, when he was still stretched out under a hedge, he heard a treading noise behind him. He turned to see a huge vulture stalking him. These scavenger birds can have a wingspan of seven feet when in flight. Its ugly head with its impersonal eyes and scythe-like beak seemed to be set on making a meal of Bob. Bob duly shot the vulture.

"I suppose it was tired of eating dog meat," Bob remarked.

Bob was amazed when, towards the end of the third day, he encountered another vulture. He was again lying under a hedge when he turned his head and this time a *huge* vulture was stalking him. It was much bigger than the first one; it had a long, thick yellow neck and neat rows of feathers from the bottom of its neck down to its big claws. It was looking down its menacing beak at him. He remembers that, although he was frightened, he could see that it was a beautiful creature.

Nevertheless, Bob wasted no time in shooting it. It collapsed in a bundle of feathers and Bob quickly slithered from under the hedge and got away. The following day he went back to the spot and was surprised to see that there was no sign of the vulture, not even a feather. He hoped that his shot had not killed the bird; that it had just been stunned and slightly wounded and was able to take off. Such a magnificent creature! Now he had more appreciation of vultures when he looked up and saw them soaring in languid circles so high in the sky.

A BREN-CARRIER INCIDENT

The 17th Division now moved south from Meiktila and broke the back of the last large Japanese defensive position at Payawbwe. Again, Bob's platoon was following up the company that did most of the heavy fighting to capture Payawbwe.

After all the travelling and action in which Bob and his platoon had participated, he wondered whether he was being more accepted by his men. Certainly they greeted him with big smiles but generally kept away from him, except during the normal army routines and when in action. 'Well that's all right,' Bob thought, 'I am, after all, different from them and I have been something of a loner all my life so far and we seem to have settled into a normal day-to-day sort of army routine co-operation.'

Just at that time Bob, in an incident not involving his platoon, went through a harrowing experience that could have cost him his life and which seemed, more than ever, to isolate him in the middle of the army.

The 17th Division was now moving southwards in a broad push on both sides of the railway line from Meiktila towards the capital city and port of Rangoon. In fact, General Slim had decided that since the 17th Division had been in the war in Burma from day one, it would now have the honour of capturing Rangoon, which is 320 miles from Meiktila.

Early in the southward push, Bob and his men entered on foot a large Burmese village that had earlier that day been taken by other British and Indian troops. The road went along one side of a very big open courtyard area which may well have been used as a marketplace during peacetime but which was now deserted. The men had been told to go straight along the road through the large courtyard to their bivouac area deeper in the village. To one side two officers were standing in a Jap-made trench, talking and looking at a map. Close by was a small grassy spot under some shady trees where a few wounded men were sitting. An orderly was bandaging the arm of one of the wounded. One of the officers called Bob over to the trench.

"Hey Sergeant, a Bren carrier should be coming here in a few minutes. Tell the man driving it to load these wounded onto it and take them to the field hospital at the south end of the village."

"Yes Sir," Bob said, and told his men to continue walking to the bivouac area. The officers then got out of the trench and followed Bob's men. Bob then waited for the arrival of the Bren carrier. He waited for about half an hour. The wounded were only lightly wounded and several of them walked away with the orderly. Others stood up on the grass.

The Bren carrier eventually arrived, minus its gun, and with two soldiers on board. Bob stepped into the road and held up his hand. The vehicle stopped.

"Officers have given orders for you to pick up the few wounded over there under the trees and take them to the field hospital along this road to the south."

The men saw that to get to the area indicated they would have to turn around and go back some twenty yards, but instead of turning the vehicle round sharply on the road itself, they drove the Bren carrier in a wide circle around the ground of the courtyard. This took them some time to do.

Boom! A mine exploded right under the vehicle. The whole vehicle lifted in the air and came down with a thump but, surprisingly, remained on its wheels. One of its occupants lay slumped over the steering wheel. The second one was sprawled on the back area with an arm over the side.

Bob looked around. It was getting late and there was now nobody about – not even the wounded. Realising that the truck was in the middle of a minefield, Bob went as near to the vehicle as the road would allow him to. A low, broken brick wall, six inches above ground, stretched from the road to within seven feet from the damaged vehicle. Bob took off his pack and placed it with his rifle on the edge of the road.

It was deadly quiet. All he could hear was the repeating thud of his heart. He stepped onto the narrow top of the low wall and walked carefully. He stopped at the end of the wall for a breather and looked down at the ground between wall and vehicle. He took a breath and gingerly lowered a boot onto the soil. Safe. He moved his other foot a step closer to the carrier. Safe. Slowly he managed a third step, then a fourth, then a fifth. He lifted himself onto the carrier.

He checked the pulse of each man. They were alive, unconscious but otherwise uninjured. He patted the face of the driver, hoping to wake him. It was fruitless. He put his arms around the man's chest and pulled him close to the edge of the vehicle. Carefully he put his feet on the closest two boot prints then lifted the man onto his shoulder in a fireman's lift. Then he stepped closer to the wall, aiming for each boot print.

Getting onto the low wall took more effort and concentration. Then it was a balancing act all the way along the top of the wall. He stepped onto the road, laid the man out carefully and stood for three minutes to get his breath back. Then he set off on the second journey. In another fifteen minutes he had laid out the second soldier beside his comrade. Then he went back a third time to fetch what was left of the soldiers' gear on the carrier.

When he got back, both soldiers were regaining consciousness. One of them sat up and looked around. Bob felt slightly dizzy. He put a hand to his head and also looked around. There was still no one else in the court-yard. He looked back at the two men. One man was standing and helping the other man to his feet. They stood there, regaining their equilibrium. One took a drink from his water flask then gave a drink to the other chap. They looked at the wrecked Bren carrier.

"Jesus! How the hell...?"

"Are you all right?" Bob asked.

Both soldiers nodded.

"Yea, we're all right."

The two men talked to each other and compared bruises.

"It's amazing," one of them mumbled.

One of the officers who had spoken to Bob earlier came striding along the road towards them. He looked at the patch of grass under the trees.

"Where are the wounded soldiers?" he called to Bob.

Bob shrugged, feeling the dizziness increasing. The two soldiers began picking up their gear and edging away.

"Are they at the dressing station?" the officer asked.

The two soldiers were walking away at this point

"I don't know. They were there but then I was ...." Bob managed to say.

The officer looked at Bob as though he was an imbecile, cursed under his breath, swivelled on his heel and strode back the way he'd come.

Bob watched the retreating officer then looked around the courtyard again. It was deserted. The thumping of his heart came back – the only sound in the area. He felt terribly alone. He picked up his gear and his rifle and walked to the grassy patch where the wounded men had been. It was getting dark. He felt terribly tired and disoriented. He looked through the trees and then down the road. It looked to him like a valley parted by dark walls of bamboo. Dracula-shaped shadows drifted in there and towards him. The thumping of his heart slowed and he felt faint. He curled up on the grass and fell fast asleep. But his problems were not over.

A gentle sun shone early the next morning. A few soldiers walked by and took no notice of Bob curled up and half asleep on the grass. The sound of a vehicle driving by woke Bob up fully. He sat up slowly, stood up and looked about him as though in a new world. Nobody looked at the partly wrecked Bren carrier. Two Indian soldiers walked slowly past him. He went up to them and asked where the first bivouac area was. They pointed down the road. Bob walked slowly after them.

Bob never saw or heard from the two soldiers he'd rescued. Neither did he tell anyone about the incident. That was the end of it. Soldiers are often given bravery awards when they carry the wounded off a battlefield or rescue someone from a dangerous situation. But there was no one to witness what happened on this occasion.

EXPLOSIVE DEMOTION

Bob settled with his men in the new encampment area in the village for a while. The next day McGuire came to Bob and showed him his grenade, which seemed to have a defect. The handle seemed to be loose, which could endanger anyone who pulled out the pin. The grenade would probably go off prematurely. Bob looked at the grenade, then went with McGuire to the quartermaster's temporary store. To Bob's surprise the quartermaster picked up the grenade, had a look at it, gave it back to McGuire and said, "There's nothing wrong with it. The handle is a tiny bit loose but it will release just the same. You can't replace it."

Then he turned and attended to another matter.

The next day the platoon went out on a patrol that lasted most of the day. Bob felt increasingly sick as the day wore on and when they returned to the village he had to make a dash to the latrines. Three crude latrines, barely covered by flimsy wood and canvas structures, were situated at the end of a clearing. Bob visited them several times during the night and again the next morning. At one point he walked into some surrounding bush, dug a hole and squatted down. The result was a stool of an awful bluish colour with streaks of blood on it. A short bout of giddiness came over him. He knew he would have to report to sick bay.

When he got back into the clearing, Fred and McGuire were waiting for him. They showed the grenade to Bob and urged him again to exchange it. The handle seemed to be looser than it was the previous day.

"Well I was just going to report to..." Bob began, then he decided to go to the quartermaster again. Fred went back to his tent and Bob went with McGuire across the clearing and beyond it. They arrived at the single-storey building being used as the quartermaster's store. It had two entrances on one side to the main room. Bob entered the northern entrance while McGuire remained just outside the open doorway. Bob walked in and called for the quartermaster. There was no answer. He looked back at McGuire who shrugged. Bob then walked in the room to the second entrance and called again.

"Quartermaster?"

Again no answer. There seemed to be nobody about but Bob could not see that behind a screen a man was sleeping soundly on a mattress. Bob felt a slight dizziness and the return of cramps in his stomach. He took a step outside the second door to get some fresh air.

To his surprise he saw McGuire running away from the first entrance.

"McGuire? What the...?"

Then, to his horror, he heard the hiss that a grenade makes just before it goes off. He flattened himself on the ground with his hands covering the back of his head. The grenade went off with a blast inside the building. It smashed part of the door, and a wooden wall and the counter. Bob sat up to survey the damage and realized that he was untouched by the explosion but that the sickness was overcoming him. He was conscious of shouts and running boot steps approaching him. He felt himself slipping away in a faint.

"Sergeant! What the hell's going on here?" were the last words he heard. He recovered partially. Someone helped him to the hospital area, where he reported sick and was sent immediately to hospital.

Bob was not sure how long he lay in a haze in a hospital ward with malaria and dysentery patients. A nurse informed him that he had an extreme case of hookworm and that he would have to stay in hospital for a couple of weeks.

It was two weeks before Bob was well enough to return to his unit, which was by then in another village some twenty miles further south. Looking somewhat thinner, he was ushered into an officer's mobile office.

"Did you know that a private sleeping behind a screen in the Quarter master's Store was killed by the explosion?" the officer said.

"No, I had no idea," Bob said.

To Bob's surprise and shock the officer began reading to him a written report of an inquiry that had been held about the grenade incident without his knowledge. McGuire had maintained that he was handing the grenade to Bob when it slipped out of his hand and fell to the floor. Realizing that the defective grenade would explode at any moment, he had run for his life. The inquiry found that, as the senior soldier, Bob was responsible for what happened. It concluded that Bob should have taken the grenade from McGuire well away from the building, secured it and taken it into the building himself.

"Sir, I was in hospital for two weeks recovering from a bad case of hookworm disease. How could an inquiry be held without my input? If someone had visited me in the hospital..." Bob said.

"The officers at the inquiry felt that they had all the evidence they needed. More time could not be spent on the inquiry as the whole camp was about to uproot and move further south due to the development of the war and in accordance with General Slim's orders. You hereby lose your rank of sergeant and are demoted to the rank of corporal."

Bob stared at the officer.

"That will be all," the officer concluded.

"No, that is not all," Bob said. "I refuse the rank of corporal. I will be a private soldier from here on."

And Bob walked out of the office.

Bob discovered that Fred had had the rank of sergeant bestowed on him. Bob was content with that; he knew that Fred was a good soldier and had leadership qualities. When Bob returned to his platoon he briefly congratulated Fred and then adopted the role of private as if that had always been his position. However, it was his choice to remain the quiet one, the social outsider and a good soldier. And he never referred again to the Quarter Master's store incident.

Briefly in his thoughts Bob wondered, "Surely the Quartermaster was to blame – for allowing a defective grenade to be used. Or was the clique to blame? Once they knew that they had a defective grenade in their hands, did they plan McGuire's dropping the grenade inside the quartermaster's building? Or was it a quick decision just by McGuire as soon as he saw that the quartermaster was absent? Is that why he ran away without warning Me?"

The rest of the platoon was well aware of Bob's athletic and physical prowess in spite of his short stature, and so they left him alone generally and co-operated with him in times of action and day-to-day soldier work. In any case, Bob believed, they had now achieved what they wanted – *their* man as sergeant.

There was one incident in which a man did try to test Bob's patience and that man was McGuire. Several days after Bob's return to the platoon the men were on patrol when McGuire, as if it were an afterthought, blurted out: "Hey Bob, you look naked without any stripes."

Perhaps some of the men bit their lips to stop themselves from sniggering but Bob took no notice of the remark at all. Encouraged by Bob's lack of response, McGuire decided to go further. When the men returned to their tent after the patrol, Bob was the last one to enter. The others were sitting or lying down. Bob walked to his ground sheet and bedding and began to adjust it. McGuire began to hum and then sing softly, but gradually getting louder:

> "Hush little baby don't you cry
> Mama's going to buy you a brand new stripe
> And if that stripe gets taken away
> Mama's gonna buy you a brand new army
> And if that army is taken away ...."

Young Greg and a couple of the others chuckled.

With an expressionless face, Bob straightened from his ground sheet and took a couple of slow steps that brought him close to McGuire.

McGuire continued: *"Mama's going to buy you a..."*

Bob gave McGuire one swift straight punch to the jaw. Clunk! McGuire flopped to the floor, out cold. Bob then looked straight at the others. They were all very quiet. Bob turned and went back to adjust his bedding. Nobody nettled Bob again.

Why did Bob not use this method to pull the men of his platoon into line when he was sergeant? Well, there was no open defiance or antagonism against him when he was sergeant; the men went along with him in whatever had to be done but kept an eye open for "safe" opportunities to let Bob find himself in some sort of trouble.

Had the grenade explosion been planned by the clique, or at least by Fred and McGuire? Bob spent a lot of time thinking it over. He believes it was. And unfortunately Bob's falling so sick just at that time made the outcome easier for them – the installing of their man as platoon sergeant. It would have been even easier for them had Bob been killed.

THE COMFORT OF TEA

One common thing that identifies an Englishman is his love of a cup of tea. I watched a TV story one day about Jamaicans settling in England. A Jamaican woman was terribly upset because she was unable to get a job despite her good qualifications. Her Jamaican boyfriend, who had been in the country longer than she had, said "When you're very upset here, you must do what the English do. You have a nice cup of tea."

We remember Bob saying how a hot cup of tea did wonders when he'd been doing hours of sentry work in cold, windy, rainy weather on the railway line on the west coast of Cumbria. He experienced the same "up-liftment" every time he was able to have a mug of tea in India and Burma, especially after a long trek through jungle or arid plain. He once heard one of his men say that in those conditions a mug of tea was better than a shot of whiskey. He said, however, that tealeaves were part of his rations and that he usually made his own tea, by boiling water in a can over a small fire of dried bamboo sticks. "Bamboo is amazing fuel," he said. "It does not let off smoke."

Ken Cooper said that to every platoon "the eternal life-giving tea was a priority. Each section carried a blackened 7lb jam tin in which was a netting bag of damp tea leaves." During long treks in Burma the soggy tea leaves lost quite a lot of their flavour but remained just as welcome.

George MacDonald Fraser earned a reputation for brewing the best tea in his platoon so almost the first thing he did whenever his section took a break while on patrol was to brew some good tea for his men.

Bernard Fergusen in his excellent book on his time with the Chindits, *Beyond The Chindwin,* mentions several times the welcome good taste and relief that came with the tea-breaks from the hazardous mission through the jungle, even on the hottest, sweltering days.

The same sentiment was expressed by Australians fighting the Japanese in New Guinea on the infamous Kokoda Trail. An exhausted Syd Heylen of the 39th Australian Battallion, said, "I know the nicest thing I ever had on the Kokoda Trail was a cup of tea given to me by the Salvation Army who followed us – no milk, no sugar, just half a cup, that's all they had. I never forgot that one." [19]

As we have seen, Bob often made his own tea – he preferred it that way. So even the tea break was not an occasion for comradeship for Bob.

LETTERS FROM HOME

While his platoon was moving deep into Burma, Ken Cooper noted that when a man was carrying a letter he had received a short while before, "It was a revelation to see the change that came over the man when he was savouring the presence of a letter in his pocket... So long as each felt the other was safe and well, somewhere, there was hope. Life might some day be the same again as it once had been. We dared not contemplate anything else." [20]

Bob too, was happy to receive a letter now and then from his mother, telling him of the family news. In his return letters he informed his parents about events such as his enjoyable time at Darjeeling and Gulmarg and the general progress of his company. He told them about some of the bouts of sickness he had, nothing about personal achievements and nothing about the situation between himself and the rest of his section.

ONE-TO-ONE STALKING

By late April 1945 the 17th Division was operating in an area of about fifty miles north and south of the town of Nsaunglebin. It must be understood that at this stage of the war other British and Indian forces after a hard struggle had defeated the Japanese on the Arakan Peninsular in the southwest part of Burma. So there was now a surge of broken, disorganized Japanese units and individual soldiers retreating from the peninsular and from western Burma through the land mainly towards the sector now largely controlled by the 17th Division. In other words, what was left of the Japanese army was cut in half. The western half had to cut through here in order to retreat to Malaysia to regroup with the Japanese army there. So groups like Bob's platoon had to do a lot of patrol work which involved some skirmishing with small pockets of these retreating enemy soldiers.

---

[19] Keith Murdock – Sound Archive AWM.
[20] *The Little Men* by Ken W. Cooper, pp 83 and 85.

It is perhaps the one-to-one confrontation with an enemy soldier that most soldiers do not like to experience and which emphasises most the individual soldier's feeling of aloneness that General Slim mentions in the first quote in this book. During this time Bob's platoon was moving in extended order through a field of high reeds beside a stream. Because Bob was not tall, his wading through the parting and closing wall of reeds was unnerving. He would not have known a Jap was near until he came right upon him. Eventually, however, they broke through the high reed area onto a clear grassless stretch beside the stream.

"OK, we'll take a break here," Fred said, "Greg, you're on guard."

Young Greg groaned but went to a slightly higher side and took up his position. A couple of the others went to the stream to refill their water flasks. The others sat down and chatted quietly and lit up cigarettes, something Bob would not allow in such a position when he was sergeant. That smoke could easily give their position to any enemy, Bob thought.

Always restless, Bob remained on his feet and paced slowly around the group, always peering into the surrounding reeds. At one point he slipped quietly into the reeds and walked forward carefully, parting the way forward with bayonet and barrel. He did this almost every time the section took a break in the countryside. He was very fit; he wanted to find the enemy and outmanoeuvre him. He would tread carefully, be watchful; if a leaf quivered he'd stop and stay frozen for a few minutes if necessary, until he knew it was alright to go on.

He soon came to a fair sized clearing right in the middle of the reed area. He scanned the perimeter slowly then stepped into the clearing and walked to the middle. A sixth sense made him look to the left above the level of the reeds. He saw a Japanese soldier, probably standing on an ant heap or a rock several yards away. They were staring straight at each other in disbelief. The Jap ducked out of sight and Bob crouched down. With his heart thumping, Bob considered what to do.

There was no doubt the man would come looking for him. His first urge was to retreat to his men. No, that could endanger both him *and* his men. He moved to a different part of the perimeter and then, as quietly as he could, he slipped back into the wall of reeds. He turned, took a couple of steps backwards, knelt down and lifted his rifle to firing position, making sure that his bayonet was not protruding through the reed wall. Then he took aim at the spot where he reckoned the Japanese soldier would emerge.

Bob's heartbeat was the only sound in the universe – thud, thud, thud, thud, as he waited and waited. Presently a small section of reed near where Bob was aiming quivered and then was still again. Bob adjusted his aim. Then a rifle protruded, bit by bit. The Japanese soldier stepped into the clearing. He held his rifle in line with his shoulders but with his head raised. He stopped, stood still and moved his gaze around the perimeter, bit by bit. Bob sweated as he aimed at the man's chest and began to squeeze the trigger. The Jap's circular scanning of the perimeter stopped when it was pointing straight at Bob. Bob froze. Two seconds were an eternity. Then the Jap's gaze continued its slow-moving circular sweep.

Bob fired a single shot. The man's upper body jerked and he fell backwards onto the ground. His rifle fell away from him.

The sound to Bob was like an explosion but he kept still with his rifle in firing position. Then he studied the perimeter of the circle in case any Jap companion should come through. All was quiet. The man must be alone, Bob thought and waited another minute.

He was just rising to go forward when – boom! – an explosion in the clearing made him drop flat. A grenade thrown by a companion? No, Bob decided. He rose silently, emerged from the wall of reeds and walked quietly to the fallen man.

The man's arms were folded across his chest and his urgent, fixed stare looked like religious fervour. His hands were missing. Some shredded skin protruded from the ends of his long sleeves and into the gaping hole in his chest. His jawbone was gone. While still alive, the man had held a grenade to his chest.

Bob always took aim at the chest. He said the Japanese usually aimed for the head, but the chest was a bigger target and your shot would either kill the man or put him out of action.

The men were still in their relaxed positions when Bob returned. Some were still smoking. Only young Greg looked tense and gazed at Bob when he stepped through the reeds.

McGuire looked up at Bob. "What was all the noise about?" he said.

Bob said nothing.

"OK men," Fred said as he stood up. "Up you get. We'll move along then."

The men stood up, picked up their gear and rifles, stubbed out their cigarettes and followed Fred, who found a pathway through the reeds and onto flat land. Nobody said a thing about this time from then on.

DEATH IN A VILLAGE

When Bob looks back he admits that his habit during the latter part of the war of detaching himself from his section at times when they were on patrol was foolish and went against army recommendations since it increased one's chances of being killed by the enemy. But as he did not trust his own men, for Bob it was the preferred option. Ironically, by putting himself in danger in this way he killed more enemy soldiers than any other man in his platoon. And he never had any trouble finding his way back to the platoon.

Because the Japanese forces in the region were by now in disarray, many of its soldiers were moving in very small groups or individually. Some may have been deserters whilst others may have lost their comrades through sickness, starvation or enemy attack. Some small groups may have split up by choice, thinking this was the best way to avoid the enemy.

On another day of patrolling while "on the way to Rangoon", Bob's group was moving through an area of high grass and patches of swamp. As usual Bob followed his instincts at one point and moved parallel to but further away from the group until he was out of their sight. He was soon soaked and sweaty from the wet conditions and the heat. To his surprise he came rather suddenly upon a small village where British soldiers were setting up camp. The men were mainly truck drivers and non-combatants and some villagers. Men were walking to and fro, carrying equipment and stores into bashas. There did not seem to be any sentries on the edges of the village.

An even greater surprise for Bob was the sudden appearance of a single armed Japanese soldier who entered the scene as Bob had, through the surrounding long grass, close to where Bob was standing. Nobody but Bob looked at him. After looking in bewilderment at the busy scene about him, the Japanese soldier looked straight at Bob. Then he took off in a panic. Instead of turning and running back into the screen of long grass, he ran down a lane with native huts on both sides.

One shot from Bob killed him.

Nobody in the village seemed to take any notice. Some stared briefly at the dead man then went on with their business. Had the death of an enemy soldier become so common? Bob puzzles about that reaction to this day.

In all, Bob killed seven isolated individual Japanese soldiers. He told me that because he was so fit during those days and because he did not like the company of his section, one thing remained strong in his mind; to prove to himself that he was a better soldier than the enemy. In some of these cases it was a matter of the enemy soldier and Bob stalking each other to the end.

MONSOON SLAUGHTER

In this latter part of the war, Bob says, you went to sleep smelling death and you woke up smelling death.

In Burma the monsoon starts in the month of May and continues to the end of October. That meant it rained almost every day, sometimes in heavy downpours, at other times in soft drizzles but it was rain, rain, rain and more rain. That was one of the reasons why General Slim had wanted the advance of the British and Indian armies to be fast – to get to Rangoon before the rains. Unlike in previous wars in Burma, the fighting carried on this time during the monsoon. The soil, which was almost as hard as rock during the rest of the year, became a quagmire in the monsoon season. Vehicles had to be pulled and pushed through mud and the soldiers were permanently wet.

What if the men were too far away from base camp when night fell, especially if it was raining? They simply had to sleep on the ground. Bob would choose a piece of slightly higher ground, take his rolled up gas cape from above his backpack, unroll it on the ground, put his backpack down as a pillow, lie down, pull the excess part of the cape over his body and head and in no time he would be asleep. At times he was able to find a low bund on which he would lay his head. Luckily, the ground that was hot during the day warmed the water.

The only parts that got cold were his feet. Every half hour or so he got up, stamped his feet and walked around a bit until his feet felt warm again, then settled down again in the three inches of water.

Of course, there was always one man on watch, who would wake up the next man when his two-hour shift was over.

The monsoon rains became heavier and heavier. The retreating Japanese had blown up all bridges to slow the Allied advance towards Rangoon. The British built bailey bridges using the supports of the destroyed bridges or pontoons to create a floating bridge. In fact, the longest floating bailey bridge ever built was the one thrown over the Chindwin for the parts of the British and Allied army that converged on the Japanese to the north and west of Mandalay. But in the approach to Rangoon the monsoon rains swelled the rivers so much that they washed away most of the bailey bridges, so the progress of the 17th Division was slowed down even more. This was a pity because General Slim had given the 17th the honour of conquering Rangoon because it had been in the war from day one.

General Slim had a second string to his bow and that was a parachute and amphibious attack from the sea to squeeze the Japanese in Rangoon. With the 17th slowed down, the amphibious attack went ahead, only to find that the Japanese had abandoned Rangoon. The 17th Division had now halted about 25 miles from Rangoon but they had advanced 775 miles from Imphal to Helega in three months.

The Japanese intent now was to get as many of their soldiers as possible heading eastwards to escape to Malaysia. This did not mean that they no longer put up a fight. Wherever possible their leaders organized groups for rearguard action and attacks to halt British progress or to isolate groups of British and Indian troops.

Bob's section was largely given mop-up duties and instructions to destroy the retreating enemy. At one stage Bob and his section were stationed at a base and sent on nightly operations for several nights on the Rangoon Road. On the first day, while it was still daylight, the men, all armed with rifles, were put onto several open trucks and driven northwards. They were soon driving along a straight part of the road with what seemed like an endless swamped paddy field on both sides. The trucks stopped and all the men got off. By now it was almost dark. They were ordered to form a long line on the westward-facing side of the road, just a couple of feet from each other, to lie down and take aim as though in a firing range. It was now too dark for them to see further than about twelve feet in front of them over the flooded paddy field.

They waited and waited. Then, after about twenty minutes, they began to hear the faint sound of splashing a long way off. Their officer gave an order.

"Set sights to one hundred yards!"

They all did so in the direction of the distant splashing sounds.

"Take aim."

They did so.

"Fire!"

The volley from the long line of soldiers was deafening. The officer waited a minute, then his orders followed.

"Reload."

"Take aim."

"Fire!"

The procedure seemed to go on endlessly. Then the officer waited for a longer time while they all listened. It was dead quiet. The men were allowed to sit or stand up to stretch stiff and weary limbs for about ten minutes. Then the sound of splashing of feet or boots in the paddy field started again, at first quietly, in dribs and drabs and then more loudly. The officer ordered the men down and the same controlled shooting procedure continued for another good twenty minutes. This carried on all night with a light rain falling all the time.

When they could see further in the early morning, the shooting stopped. And so did the rain. The men all pulled themselves up, massaged their stiff limbs or walked a few feet along the road to stretch their legs. A couple of trucks away from Bob two officers were conferring. Bob stepped into the paddy field and the water came up nearly to his knees. Fred followed him.

"I'm curious to see what we were shooting at," Bob said.

Fred hesitated but said, "OK, I'll go with you... but just a short way."

A close mist had come with the morning and still blocked their westward view. The two men fixed bayonets and trudged along in the water. The wall of mist receded before them as they went.

Suddenly they walked into a bigger break in the mist and stood still. Before them was an appalling sight. The bodies of dead Japanese soldiers were scattered everywhere. Some lay face down in the water, some face up. All had at least one bullet hole visible on back, chest or head. One had a wound in the middle of his thigh and, judging from the amount of mud he had gouged up from the ground and onto his chest, he had drowned while trying to keep his head above water. Another lay stretched out on the bodies of two comrades, on whom he must have crawled to stay above the water, only to die from loss of blood. The British had discovered that this area was an escape route where thousands of Japanese were trying to cross at night.

Bob and Fred stared at the carnage about them. Then Fred gestured to Bob with his head that they should go back. As they turned, they heard the familiar feet-splashing sounds coming towards them. They took aim at the direction of the sounds. Two figures emerged to one side of them, holding rifles and heading eastwards, unaware of Bob and Fred. Bob indicated which one he would fire at and he and Fred fired. Both Japanese soldiers collapsed and lay still in the water.

Bob and Fred looked carefully about them, then Fred turned and walked back towards the road. Bob was just about to turn when another, urgent-sounding splashing came towards him, and through the mist cover a hunched figure charged straight at him. With no time to shoot, Bob let the figure come almost onto him, then bayoneted him right into the head. Bob pulled the bayonet out as the body slumped to the ground. Then he followed Fred.

Bob did not wipe the blood from the bayonet. When he checked the blade the next morning, he found that the blood had visibly rusted or eroded part of it.

It was about this time in Bob's narrating to me that he expressed some sympathy for the common Japanese soldier.

"Man, they had a terrible time of it," he said. "Communication lines gone, starving, diseased, they were trying to walk hundreds of miles to escape."

Bob remembers another incident concerning a young officer during one of these Rangoon Road nights. His group was stationed along a road facing the west as usual. On this occasion the road was higher above the paddy fields than usual and the water, which was about four inches deep, drained eastwards towards and through a large culvert under the road. Bob's group was lined up quite near one side of the culvert. During a pause in their controlled shooting, Bob saw a group of Japanese soldiers emerge from the dark and head towards the culvert. He was astonished to see that the nearest British soldier to the Japs was a new young officer who, with his trouser legs rolled up, was busy, with his flashlight on, picking leeches off his legs.

The Japanese must have been so intent on heading eastwards that they did not notice the clear target that the officer presented. Bob's men quickly converged on the road at the top of the culvert and shot the Japs as they entered and exited the culvert.

After that first night of firing into the paddy field, the men were trucked back to base. They were able to have a shower at that particular village. First, they took off their rain-sodden clothes. Then they dealt with leeches stuck to their legs and arms. The men held lit cigarettes against them until they sizzled and dropped off. Bob was a non-smoker but he soon found that when he smeared mosquito cream or suntan cream on them they writhed and fell off. Some men had ticks on their bodies as well. When they pulled ticks off, they had to make sure with the tip of a knife to dig the tick's head out, or it would fester in the skin and create a nasty, pus-filled sore.

That evening the men were back on the road, lining up on the roadside. The usual rain limited their view but they could see further out than the previous evening over the paddy fields. Suddenly, in the distance at the left side edge of their field of vision, they saw a large number of ghostly figures. Someone shouted a warning and fired a hasty shot in that direction. The men all raised their rifles, anticipating the order to shoot. There was a faint shout from the distant figures but then they disappeared from sight.

"Hold your fire!" An officer ordered as he scanned the area with his binoculars. They all continued to stare but there was no more sign of life there.

"Nothing. Can't see anything," the officer said.

It was almost dark and the rain continued. The men were ordered down on the ground again.

"Load rifles!" the officer ordered, and the night's activity occurred just as it had the previous night.

At daybreak the men stood up, stamped their feet and moved their limbs about to combat stiffness. Some began to board the trucks.

A distinct series of cries pierced the air. Most of the men ran back to the edge of the road with rifles at the ready. The officer was quick to use his binoculars.

"Don't shoot! Don't shoot!" he shouted. "They're not Japs but who are they?"

The large group of grey figures they had briefly spotted the previous evening on the left edge of the paddy field now emerged, striding towards them, splashing through the paddy field. They were shouting and waving their arms.

"Good God!" the officer with the binoculars shouted, "They're prisoners of war! Our men!"

Bob could now make out the details: the tattered remains of khaki uniforms, the skeletal chests, the thin arms and legs, some scraggy beards. A couple of them collapsed into the water. The British soldiers dropped their guns and ran forward to meet their comrades.

Some of the prisoners cried as they embraced their saviours, others laughed and shouted and shook hands gleefully. Some soldiers lifted up weak men, carried them carefully and put them down in the back of the trucks. Bob unhooked his water bottle and gave a drink to a man with very cracked lips. He took deep swigs, belched and laughed as he gave it back to Bob. Bob put an arm around him and led him to a truck.

"You'll be in time for breakfast chum," Bob said.

"Breakfast? What's that?" the man said and laughed again.

"Where did you chaps come from?" Bob asked.

"Our guards disappeared so we walked all the way from Rangoon."

Another prisoner leant over to Bob.

"Been there for three years," he said, then he gestured at the group. "This is about a third of our original number."

Bob helped the two of them onto the truck.

This slaughter by Bob's group of men that they couldn't even see was matched by other groups in daylight fighting situations. Major John Randle, the officer Commanding B (Pathan) Company of the 7th and 10th Baluch Regiment (Indian soldiers), says in Julian Thompson's book, *Forgotten Voices of Burma*, that in a similar area it was reported to him that a strong force of Japanese soldiers on a hill called Point 99, were in a mood to surrender.

He moved with his brigade but they still had to fight their way to the top of the hill. When they got to the top they came upon a group of about 124 Japs, still armed. As the major approached, one of his men right in front of him was shot dead by a Jap. The major's soldiers immediately went mad and killed all the Japs with bayonet, grenades and Tommy guns. The major tried to take a few prisoners but his *subedar* (lieutenant) said "It's no good. You're wasting your breath." His men were on a high, adrenalin running, all steamed up. "My chaps were in a blood lust."[21]

SLAUGHTER AT THE SITTANG RIVER

If you look at the map at the front of the book you will see that a section of the last area patrolled and controlled by the 17th Division includes a section on the eastern side of the Sittang River. General Slim wanted to smash the Japanese army so that little of it would be able to join the Japanese forces in Malaya and continue the war there. In fact, General Slim and his senior officers were already planning the invasion of Malaya. Bob's platoon's next mission was to join the men already stationed on the eastern side of the Sittang River in order to deal with Japanese soldiers as they crossed or attempted to cross the river in their eastwards retreat.

I will describe what happened on just one of the several days that Bob was stationed on the east side of the Sittang River. This part of the river was about a hundred yards wide. Bob was standing with several platoons all in a rough line on the riverbank looking towards the other shoreline. The river was deep and flowing at a steady pace. Officers and some of the soldiers were scanning through binoculars. Bob managed to borrow a pair from another soldier and had a good look. In one of several breaks in the vegetation on the far shoreline, where a stretch of sand jutted out a short way into the river, he spotted a Japanese officer talking animatedly to a group of thin-looking soldiers. Each soldier had his rifle slung across his back. When the officer finished talking to them, each soldier went to a pile of canon shells that were on the beach, picked up one and held it across his chest with one arm. He then picked up a bamboo pole with his free hand. Bob had seen these poles or branches; several had washed up onto the eastern shore. They were blocked on each end to prevent the pole from sinking. Each soldier, thus laden, walked into the river. He pushed the pole under the arm that was holding the shell across his chest and then began to paddle with his free arm. Some made better headway than others. Some of them let go of the shell very soon as they struggled across. One or two even unslung the rifle from their backs as well and released it in the water.

---

[21] *Forgotten Voices of Burma* by Julian Thompson, p.35.

Some tired quickly, drifted downstream and made no effort to swim across. Some soon lost their bamboo poles and sank beneath the surface. Then several of the British soldiers started shooting with rifles, picking off the Japanese that had made headway across the river. Soon all the soldiers except Bob were shooting. It went on like this all morning: Japanese soldiers entering the water, swimming or drowning and being shot in the water. Bob was holding a Tommy gun which had been issued to some of the British soldiers, but he did not use it until much later in the day.

One of the officers told Bob that there were many crocodiles about a mile downstream that must have been having a feast. The shooting carried on in the afternoon as well. Bob never saw a single swimmer make it to the eastern shoreline.

Bob heard later that another platoon of British soldiers further upstream saw a Japanese officer march onto a sandspit leading a group of about twenty men. They all stopped at his command but remained at attention. The officer surveyed the scene before him for a few minutes, then seemed to lecture his men for a few more minutes. Then he gave a command and the whole group, including the officer, marched smartly straight into the river. As the foremost men found no more footing they continued to make the motions of marching. They were swept downstream in ones and twos. For a while only their heads or helmets could be seen then these went down. In the end they all disappeared.

When it began to get dark, Bob tired of the shooting and took a walk downstream. After a few minutes he was well away from any British soldiers. In a small enclave he came across a dead Japanese soldier lying half out of the water. He was still clutching his bamboo pole.

Bob then looked out over the river, which was narrower in this part. He could clearly see two bodies drift past. Within two minutes two more bodies drifted by. Then three went by. Another post of British troops in a few days counted over six hundred bodies floating down the river from one of the main Japanese crossing places upstream.

One group, the 12 and 13 Japanese Naval Guard Forces from the port and shore Establishments of the Imperial Navy in Burma, amounting to about twelve hundred men, lost heavily all the way on their overland journey until only three men escaped across the Sittang.[22]

---

[22] *Defeat Into Victory* by Field-Marshal Sir William Slim, pp.527-8.

THE BURNING PYRE

After Bob had stood watching the bodies floating by, he turned and walked further downstream. As he approached a batch of tall reeds, half in and half out of the water, he was surprised by a sodden Japanese soldier who burst from the reeds. He was carrying a rifle. When he saw Bob he stopped and stared. Bob pointed the Tommy gun at him.

"Surrender!" Bob shouted, but the man turned and ran away from the river. Bob let off a hasty burst that missed the man. He cursed and fired another burst more carefully. The man was riddled with bullets and fell flat on his face. Bob walked up to the man, made sure he was dead, then moved on downstream.

Any British, Gurkha or Indian soldier knew that if he came across an armed Japanese soldier he had to shoot him on sight. There had been cases where a Japanese soldier had raised arms in surrender then whipped out a revolver or a grenade to use against his would-be captor. Almost all of them refused to surrender. To them to surrender was a sign of cowardice. Bob at least gave this Jap a chance to surrender. Most Allied soldiers would have shot him on sight.

Bob walked on, keeping a wary eye open for any other man who may have made it across the river. Soon he stopped and sniffed the air. He saw smoke rising from the other side of a small grove of trees. It was semi-dark now as he made his way around the grove.

When he got to the other side he stopped. He saw a huge square pyre of dead Japanese soldiers piled neatly in about ten layers. A couple of Indian soldiers and several Burmese 'coolies' – a clean-up crew – were heaving a last corpse onto the pyre. Empty petrol cans had been placed well away from the stack. One Burmese man set the pyre alight with a burning torch. The flames spread and licked quickly right up the sides of the square until the top was also burning fiercely. Bob held his nose against the stench of burning flesh but his eyes were fixed on the scene in morbid fascination. It was a huge, neat bonfire; the flames kept to the limits of the square and roared upwards, never outwards. Suddenly, as the muscles of one of the burning corpses on the top contracted, the body sat upright in an aura of pale flame and seemed to stare in accusation at Bob.

"This is all your fault!" the eyes seemed to say.

Bob gulped, took a step backwards, then turned and walked away.

JAPANESE PRISONERS

Bob walked away from the burning pyre, reached the track that led back to the camp, slowed down and looked around as he went. All activity along the riverbank had stopped. The only sound he could hear was the footfall of his own boots.

Then he stopped and listened. Some rustling of vegetation came from the side of the road. He pointed his Tommy gun in that direction. All was quiet. Then the rustling came again. The figure of a man emerged from the brush and came onto the road some fifteen yards away, turned and plodded towards Bob. The man had no rifle and carried his boots.

"Halt! Stay right there!" Bob commanded.

The man stopped and peered at Bob. The man's shirt was in tatters. His trousers were partly rolled up and partly cut away. His exposed legs were as thick as tree trunks and the skin was stretched tight while blood oozed from a myriad of sores and cracks. The man's eyes were bloodshot and watery. This man had *beriberi*, caused by deficiency of vitamins; it commences with peripheral oedema (swelling in the limbs) and oozing of blood and pus from cracks in the stretched skin.

The man swayed a little as he stood, looking glassily at Bob. Just when Bob began to wonder what on earth he was going to do with his first captive, a military truck came along the track, heading in the direction of the camp. Bob waved the truck down and asked the two men inside it to take him and the Japanese man to the field hospital at the camp. Bob and one of the occupants of the truck helped the sick man onto the back of the truck; in fact, they really had to lift him onto it, trying as best they could not to get into contact with the suppurating, swollen legs. Bob climbed onto the back of the truck as well and sat facing the sick man all the way.

At the field hospital Bob and the other occupant helped the prisoner off the truck and Bob led him, plodding along painfully, into the hospital where he handed him over to medical personnel, knowing the man would be treated as well as any sick or wounded British soldier. At their parting, Bob looked for any sign, perhaps of gratitude, from his only prisoner, but the look in the man's eyes showed only bewilderment mixed with pain.

As Bob emerged from the tent hospital, another truck drew to a halt close to him. A commotion was going on in the back. Two British soldiers appeared to be grappling with a Japanese soldier. A third soldier got out of the cab and helped the other two forcibly take the man off the truck. Bob could see by the man's tunic that he was an officer. His hands were tied together, half his shirt had been ripped away and bloody bandages hung from his shoulders and his back. When the soldiers had shoved and dragged the resisting Jap officer into the tent hospital Bob approached the driver.

"Why the hands tied together?" Bob asked him.

"Every time we bandaged him, he ripped the bandages off. He'd rather die than be treated well by his enemy," the driver said.

As a rule, only wounded Japanese officers were taken prisoner. Most officers died in battle or committed *hara-kiri* when they faced capture, as did many soldiers. When Japanese troops were retreating from the Imphal Plain, some of their officers deserted their troops in order to save themselves. This added to the confusion of the mass retreat. Their leaders told their men that they would be maltreated, tortured and killed if captured.

Beside the large hospital tent was a smaller tent with a roped off area in front of it where a small group of about six Japanese prisoners were seated. They were not tied or shackled in any way. A few Indian guards were stationed along the roped-off area. A British army cook appeared from within the tent with a large tray on which stood six wooden bowls of rice and meat stew. He placed the tray on the only trestle table in front of the prisoners.

"Come and get it!" he said to the silent prisoners as he indicated the food to them.

At first they just sat with sullen faces. The aroma of the stew must have reached the nostrils of two of them, who stood up slowly, looked at each other then walked slowly to the table. Encouraged by signs from the cook, they each took a bowl and returned to their spot on the ground and started eating ravenously. Two more followed. Then the last two. The last man to pick up his bowl wept openly and made signs of gratitude to the cook.

"Don't mention it," said the cook, "I'm just sorry the wine steward is not on duty tonight."

NO ROOM FOR CARELESSNESS

A small number of Japanese soldiers had been able to get across the Sittang river at night. Perhaps it was for this reason that Bob's platoon was given the task of planting grenade mines along a stretch of flat land close to the eastern bank of the river. Each man was given a spot a "safe" distance away from the next man, where he dug a hole and inserted a coiled spring secured to a flat iron base. He pushed the spring flat so that it clipped shut in its suppressed position against the flat iron base. He then placed a grenade on top of the coiled spring. Next, he attached the end of a thin nylon string securely to the clip of the spring and to the grenade in such a way that it held down the lever of the grenade. Then, keeping parallel to the river, he ran the loose end of the string at a height of six to eight inches above the ground for about eight to ten feet from the grenade trap where he tied it securely to an iron stake driven into the ground and hidden by a bush or some sort of vegetation. Once he was satisfied that his trap was all in order, he would delicately remove the pin from the grenade. Of course, the grenade would not go off because of the string holding its lever down. But should a person bump or break the stretch of string, the spring and the grenade handle would be released. The spring would push the grenade upwards so that it would explode at about chest level.

From start to finish this was a delicate operation, requiring full concentration. Fred stood a safe distance away near the river and watched his men at work. Bob was the next man to McGuire's right and young Greg was the next man to McGuire's left as the men worked. Each man's spot was probably reasonably safe but the men had been instructed to fall flat away from their own string should they think that any of the other grenade traps may be about to go off prematurely. In fact, each man had to measure his safe area on which to dive in the event of an imminent explosion.

Complete silence reigned. Then, to Bob's surprise, McGuire began to speak.

"Hey Fred, isn't this a waste of time? The war's over for the nips anyway," he said.

"Shut up McGuire! Concentrate!" Fred said immediately.

"What do you think Greg?" McGuire carried on, "Some among us are even starting to save the nips instead of..."

McGuire was crouched over his booby trap having just pulled the pin out of his grenade. He twisted to look at Greg. This action caused one of his boots to slide just enough to push against the stretch of nylon string. For a split second there was a look of total terror on McGuire's face before his body was enveloped in the explosion.

Everyone fell flat. Nobody else was hurt. Greg was the first one to approach the wrecked body of McGuire. He fell to his knees and cried in anguish.

"Oh God no! Oh God no! Oh God no!"

Amazingly, McGuire was the only man in Bob's platoon to die in the war. One could say that this fortuitous event was a just outcome for the fact that McGuire was the one who gave the most trouble to Bob and the one Bob considered to be the leader of the group that had been against him. However, Bob did not reason thus. He simply considered McGuire's demise as caused by extreme carelessness and irresponsibility, since it had put his fellow soldiers at risk.

THE END OF THE WAR

The war ended on 14th August 1945 after the Americans had dropped atomic bombs on Hiroshima and Nagasaki.

The rest of Bob's Company sailed home from Rangoon. Before they departed, Bob got word that his brother Eric was in Calcutta for a while, on his way to join the occupation forces in Japan. So Bob did not leave from Rangoon with his unit. He took leave to go to Calcutta to see his brother. He then sailed home via the Suez Canal.

If the atomic bombs had not been used, there would have been a couple of million American casualties and at least three times that number of Japanese. The latest research indicates that both the Emperor and the highest Japanese military leaders would not have surrendered if the bombs had not been not dropped. They were preparing the whole population to fight to the end – with pitchforks and bamboo spears if necessary.

HOME SWEET HOME

When Bob disembarked from the ship at Liverpool he overheard some dock workers say: "Look at this bloody lot! Here's more competition for our jobs now."

The relatively small crowd welcoming the troops back from Burma were largely relations and friends of the military men. The Germans had signed the papers for their unconditional surrender on May 7th 1945. Japan signed its surrender documents on 7th September 1945.

The huge jubilation in England when the war with Germany ceased was now over. The bulk of British focus during the war had been in Europe, naturally, since Britain's very freedom and soil had been threatened from Europe, while her will to regain the same freedoms for other European countries was as strong. Britain's participation in the war in the east, however, was largely to restore Burma as part of its empire. This was a "far away" concept. No wonder the war in Burma became known as The Forgotten War, even though the outcome was Japan's biggest defeat on land in the war.

Bob's photo of 9th Battalion, The Border Regiment at Shillong, just before leaving for the war zone.

One could argue that the Allied victory in Burma paved the way to restoring Burma to the Burmese people and that was in the minds of many of her soldiers including Bob's mind. However, Britain was, in actual fact, regaining her colony. She would, of course, within a short space of time move in the direction of restoring Burma to self-rule. All in all, all this was not something close to the hearts of British citizens. Consequently, the British soldiers who returned to England after the Burma war received a very low-key welcome.

Bob was demobilized at Barrow-in-Furness. He was given a suit to wear and a rail pass. Like most people at the time, Bob's parents did not own a motor car, so Bob travelled by train to Kendal, where his parents now lived. He was welcomed warmly by his parents but hardly any other person took any notice of his return. Some 'Welcome Home' government functions were organized in towns not too far from his home but Bob was never notified of them.

There was just one occasion when he and two other lads were invited to supper by a retired couple in his former home town of Kirby Lonsdale. It was an enjoyable supper but it was the only sign, apart from that of his own family, that Bob experienced as a welcome back to his country. Nobody ever came up to him and shook his hand or said, "You chaps did well out there."

No wonder the 14th was called "The Forgotten Army"; when the men returned, they found a dreadful ignorance everywhere about the 14th Army and Burma.

There were two more examples of the sort of "welcome" that Bob received once back in England. When he visited Kirby Lonsdale he walked through the town and the same old men who had shouted at him outside a pub before the war saw him and shouted, "Where have you been all this time Bob?" Bob chose to ignore the men and walked on.

Bob was lucky enough to get another job as a carpenter on construction sites. One day the manager strolled up to Bob and started a conversation with him. When the manager asked Bob how he was getting on since the war, Bob said, "Fine, thank you. I am saving money and getting a mortgage to build my own house."

"What? The manager replied. "The likes of you shouldn't be owning a house!" Then he mumbled, "What's the world coming to?" and walked away – an illustration of the lingering class system.

To rub salt into the wound, while Bob was engaged in the building of his house, the government taxed him so heavily with "taxes for new mortgages" that it took away nearly all the soldiers' pay he had earned since he had been in the army.

No wonder Bob emigrated with his wife to Canada!

Here is one after-effect of the war: on his first night at home he was sitting in the lounge with his mother. He sniffed the air and said, "What's that smell, Mother?"

"Oh, as a welcome-home dinner, your Dad is cooking a pheasant in the oven for you."

Bob put his hand to his mouth and rushed out into the garden, where he vomited. The smell was just like the smell of the burning flesh on the tall pyre of burning Japanese soldiers that he had come across in Burma. It took Bob some time to readjust his nostrils to the smell of cooking meat.

Bob's father was a survivor of the First World War and a policeman and although he cooked his son a meal when he arrived home, he did not speak to him for some time because Bob had lost his stripes.

Back in England, the happiest time for Bob was when he met Jean Miller, originally from Blackburn, Lancashire, at a Service Club social evening in Kendal. She did three years training as a physical education teacher before working in her parent's hardware store. They were married on 4th August 1949 and immigrated to Vancouver, British Columbia, Canada in 1954.

In Vancouver Bob worked in construction for many years and as soon as he was able to do so, bought a house at 2659 Marine Drive, West Vancouver. Over the years he improved the house with his own hands, getting hold of inexpensive materials and using them so that the finished product – be it a renovated bedroom, an altered kitchen or banisters on the staircase – turned out so smart that it looked as if he had used expensive materials. He took more than one job in a day. For some time he did woodwork teaching at West Vancouver High School at night.

Bob's brothers Stanley and Eric are both deceased. Bob has two sons – Ian, who lives in Vancouver and Don, who lives in Kelowna – both towns being in British Columbia. He has two grandchildren, Tyler and Sarah, who both live in Vancouver.

A footnote: There was just one more occasion when Bob used his lethal right fist. In the first few years in West Vancouver, he and Jane rented a cottage in an area with many cottages owned by a landlord. One day there was a loud knocking on Bob's front door. He opened the door to find a tenant from another cottage shouting at him, waving his hands almost in Bob's face and complaining incoherently about something. Bob can't even remember what the man's complaint was about. As the man almost shoved himself onto Bob, Bob put an end to the performance with one very hard, straight, right punch. The man went down and it was a while before he revived.

The owner of the cottages requested that Bob and Jane leave their cottage. As Bob and Jane were about to purchase their house on Marine Drive, Bob was happy to go.

In 2010 Bob sold the house and moved with Jean to a West Vancouver apartment overlooking the sea. Every year Bob takes part in the West Vancouver War Memorial Parade in his military uniform with the slouch hat he wore in India and Burma.

THE ORDINARY JAPANESE SOLDIER

By the end of the war 150,000 Japanese soldiers had been killed. Only 1,700 had been taken prisoner and of these only 400 were not ill or wounded when taken. No one above the position of major was taken prisoner. On the other hand, 250,000 Burmese civilians died during the war and there were about 70,000 Allied soldier casualties[23] – a huge destruction of human life.

When Bob saw the many corpses floating down the Sittang River and the huge pyre of burning corpses, these showed him what war reduces mankind to. It was soon after this that Bob came across the Japanese soldier afflicted with beriberi. Bob could have shot him on the spot but instead chose to take him prisoner. Here was a chance to show some compassion for an enemy.

"The ordinary Jap soldiers had a hell of a tough time of it."

Bob made this remark several times during the course of telling me his story. Plunged into a war by reckless leaders, ultimately deserted by their officers, supply and communication lines gone, hundreds of miles to trek on foot through jungles, exposed open landscape and across rivers, starving and diseased and constantly harassed by a well-supplied and mechanised enemy from land and air, the defeated Japanese certainly learned what it was like to be on the receiving end of total warfare.

Bob did not share such sentiments with his fellow soldiers but neither did it stop him being an effective soldier himself.

THE CLIQUE AND BOB

The leaders of the British war effort in India and Burma were full of praise for the British soldier in that campaign.

---

[23] Estimated from Wikipedia.

Here is one example:

> *"They were fine men, sure of who they were and of the officers who led them. They loved their country and returned to it with such joy. I did not know one of them who did not."*[24]

The incredible stand made by the British and allied soldiers at Kohima gives justification for these words from Colonel Richards but I don't think they are words that apply to *all* British soldiers in that war – as Bob surely found out.

Max Hastings says in *Nemesis* that the British army in Burma functioned according to the British class system, namely that the officers were always supplied with a good mess wherever possible while the ordinary soldier had to resort to bars and brothels of notable squalor for his entertainment when on leave, something that Bob noticed very plainly.

It is interesting at this point to notice the official code of behaviour expected of the British soldier:

APPROPRIATE BEHAVIOUR
Our job depends on -
1. *Not offending others*
2. *Putting other's needs before our own*
3. *Honesty*
4. *Supporting your teammates*
5. *The army needs a demanding standard of social behaviour from you.*

These points are more idealistic than practical in the real situation of soldiers at war, yet Bob came close to fulfilling these precepts.

As a non-drinker, a non-smoker and a non-swearer, throughout the war Bob was automatically "a man alone" among his fellow soldiers, especially as he grew up that way, strengthening himself and finding his way so independently. Even in sports, he excelled in individual activities. In rugby, he was a boy playing with men, out on the wing where he could play on the outside of the main body of the team.

Bob was made platoon sergeant by officers who saw his soldiering abilities and surely, his potential leadership qualities. Looking back, Bob concluded that he was better at carrying out orders than giving them. In

---

[24] Garrison Commander at Kohima, Colonel Hugh Richards.

fact, an officer who had had a hand in training Bob in India and who witnessed some of the action in which Bob had taken part, came across Bob's father in Kendall before Bob was back home from the war and told him that Bob was the finest soldier who had served under him. Unfortunately Bob's father could not remember the officer's name when Bob got back home. I would not be surprised if the officer was Lieutenant-Colonel John Petty.

I conclude that it was simply incredibly bad luck that Bob landed in that particular group of men. He described them to me as having "smiles on their faces but murder in their hearts". What he saw of other British soldiers did not impress him either. In fact, he told me that outside actual war action, "the common British soldiers were an awful lot."

Other soldiers no doubt found him aloof, unsociable, taciturn. Yet he was probably the best individual soldier in his group. He assures me that he wanted to be a soldier; he enjoyed being a soldier (but not the company of his men) and wanted to do the best he could. So there could have been a certain amount of envy on their part. Yet all this does not excuse or explain why the men went as far as they did in their disregard for and treatment of him. I believe that Bob's assertion is true – that to the men the war was secondary. They were a complacent clique, in this case of Catholics, who looked after themselves and believed they could act with subtle impunity against an outsider whom they considered to be in their way.

Since I have touched on the matter of religion within a platoon, it is interesting to note these refreshing words that Ken Cooper heard from two of his men, both protestants, after a battlefield funeral service:[25]

"Hey, did you know that priest was a Holy Roman?"

"Don't care a bugger. As far as I'm concerned it don't matter if he's RC, Parsee or bleeding Khaki. He stayed and buried our lads, didn't he?"

In the army, each company was split into three platoons. Each platoon was commanded by a lieutenant assisted by a sergeant. Each platoon had three sections of about ten men, usually consisting of a corporal, a lance-corporal, a Bren gunner and seven riflemen.

As sergeant, Bob was to support the officer in charge of the whole platoon but he was also assigned basically to the "clique' section. As we have seen, Lieutenant John Petty was Bob's lieutenant from the time of the stay

---

[25] From *The Little Men* by B.W. Cooper.

at Darjeeling and he and Bob got along well. However Lt Petty was promoted away from the platoon quite early in the platoon's progress in the war. Thereafter, the new lieutenants were usually relatively inexperienced. Two of them were killed and it took some time for them to be replaced. Others left platoon matters to Bob.

Bob believed that the clique influenced the rest of the platoon to hold him in poor regard. When demoted to private he had to stay in the same section.

It is interesting to compare Bob's experience with his section with that of the writer, George MacDonald Fraser, whose magnificent book, *Quartered Safe Out Here* is his recollection of his time in the 9th Battalion of the 17th Division in the Burma War. Fraser and Bob were in different companies. Fraser was the youngest man in his section and Bob was one of the youngest in his section. Fraser does not talk about action before the battle around Meiktila, so I presume he joined his platoon when it started moving from Imphal in mid-July 1944, in pursuit of the Japanese in retreat. At that time Bob had already been active against the Japanese since before November 1943.

Fraser was a Scotsman who had moved to Carlisle in Cumbria where he was educated and where he joined a Cumbrian regiment consisting of men from his own area around Carlisle. Fraser immediately took to his fellow soldiers in his section. As a writer he familiarised himself with their rough ways and dialect and, even as the youngest and least experienced among them, he earned their respect as much as he respected them. They were a bunch of interesting, swearing, sometimes bullying, sometimes thieving (not against their own section) men yet they were as loyal and steadfast and dependable as any group could be. When Fraser became their corporal, he describes an occasion when his section was sent out to collect the parachute drops from the RAF. Fraser was impressed by their enthusiasm for the job and later learned that they had ingeniously stolen a whole lot of food and items for their section's 'stash', which they shared for some time afterwards. His men had taken as many *chaguls*[26] with them, apparently filled with water but actually empty and they had filled them with their pickings. He says he learned that such practise was almost a tradition in the 17th Division. He was amused by it, even admired the men for their

---

[26] *chaguls* – canvas water bags that keep water cool through condensation.

resourcefulness and saw it as just a part of the colourful, rough but admirable make-up of his fellow soldiers. Bob, on the other hand, considered such action as depriving one's fellow soldiers.

Fraser was with at least two of the men in his section who were killed during a charge into an enemy position. That sort of experience must bond a man to his section or platoon even further. Although Bob and the men in his section and platoon were indeed in several dangerous, life-threatening situations, there was only one death during the war in Bob's platoon, namely, that of McGuire in the grenade trap incident.

Fraser came from the same town or area as the men in his platoon. The men from Bob's section were largely from industrial parts of Lancashire so coming from different areas was perhaps the first divide between Bob and his men.

In his magnificent book *When All Hell Broke Loose* Max Hastings says that the "mate-ism" among Australian soldiers in the same platoon was a far more binding force than any concept of patriotism or large moral purpose – the very concepts that were embedded in Bob and whose absence in his men he deplored. On the other hand, any "mate-ism" among the clique was of a shallow nature. This helps us to understand the unfortunate situation in his platoon.

In answer to some moralists in the 1990s who took a dim view of the killing fields in this latter part of the war in Burma and of the conduct of men in Fraser's section, Fraser says:

> *"You cannot, you must not, judge the past by the present; you must try to see it in its own terms and values if you are to have any inkling of it."*

I agree fully with these words of Fraser's. However, in Bob's case we have a soldier of the 1940s whose "ten commandment" principles collided with the terms and values of the war situation as applied to the common soldier at the time. Hence his situation as a man alone.

I guess one keeps on returning to the question: Why did Bob not at some stage confront the clique about their attitude/actions against him? Bob said that because he did not have irrefutable proof of the clique's actions against him he preferred to leave the matter alone, as it were, until such time as he did receive some proof in this matter or in the hope that their subtle actions against him would stop. And indeed, apart from the one incident of heckling by McGuire, it did stop once Bob became a private, but the wall between them was by that time firmly erected.

Perhaps one could say that at that time in the army's history more could have been done in the training of leadership and of co-operation within the platoon and the section but it is a fault to thrust today's thinking onto the urgency of the situation at that time.

Bob agrees with Fraser's words that the British used "the scrapings of the barrel" of her soldiers in the Burma campaign when Bob thinks of the men in his section. However, Fraser means that since the "best" soldiery was sent to fight in Europe, the achievement of the "leftovers" in India and Burma was therefore all the more remarkable.

I asked Bob how he got on with his parents before the war. He said that he was quite close to his mother but not to his father. In spite of his father's early advice to Bob to look after himself and his father's interest in Bob's rugby games Bob says his father was very strict and had a temper. He expected more of Bob. He approved more of Bob's two younger sons who went to a grammar school and did some study after school years.

Even though Bob's father cooked a pheasant for Bob upon his arrival home, from that moment onwards for quite a long time he would not speak to Bob because Bob had lost his stripes. This "distance" between him and his father could be another factor that contributed to Bob's singularity.

Bob was always one who achieved largely on his own. He received quick promotion as a young man in the army – from private to lance-corporal to sergeant, all before leaving England for the East. That was because his seniors saw his virtuous diligence, his no-nonsense application and progress as an individual soldier in training and for his initial good though perhaps impersonal dealing with other soldiers. I consider him a unique man of courage and integrity. He retained an innocence which strengthened his resolve to do the right thing, by himself if none about him did.

BOB'S INJURED TOE

In one of my visits to Bob, in August 2011, the lower part of his right foot below the knee, including ankle and foot, were heavily bandaged and the foot and ankle were in a special medical boot. It was then that he told me that shortly before going to the front in India he took part in an army soccer game. He had no boots so he wore a pair of runners. When kicking the ball on one occasion, his toe struck the hard ground and the big toe's joint was dislocated.

Although he experienced a lot of pain for some time, he decided not to report the injury. Within a few days his company was on its way to the front and the pain receded until he felt no more pain. Thereafter he ignored the injury for the rest of the war. It was only at the age of 91 that he started to experience pain again in the toe. An X-ray revealed that the joint in the toe was disjointed and a section of bone was disfigured so he had the necessary operation to remove bits of bone and put the disjointed part back in place. A little more than a month later, he was walking almost as normal.

The doctor who did the operation said that had Bob reported the injury in 1943 the army doctor would very likely have amputated the toe and Bob would then have been on his way home. Bob sensed this fact. He wanted to take part in the war. I see this all as another sign of Bob's toughness and resolve – a contrast to Brian Bentley and his selectively troublesome feet.

THE JAPANESE MILITARY PHILOSOPHY

What is it that made the Japanese individual soldier fight so fanatically, to fight to the death and never surrender? Here is a *very* simple explanation: the Buddhist thinking was in the past very much the core of Japanese spiritual thinking, namely, that a person should strive to be selfless and to seek the truth through peaceful means and to be honest and industrious. Over time, the Japanese leaders gradually made loyalty supersede truth and compassion, which is a betrayal of basic Buddhist principles. The leaders emphasized the "strive to be selfless" element in the sense that the individual was to think of himself as worthless other than his serving of the Emperor. It was an honour to do everything for the Emperor and the highest thing you could do for him and your great country was to die in battle. So, if the individual Japanese life is not important, then the enemy's life is much less important. Hence the wide-scale mistreatment and huge atrocities that occurred.

The Japanese leaders believed that they were liberating the countries that they attacked and would educate the people of those countries to follow the wonderful Japanese way of life and beliefs. However, this liberating would take place with "our swords that will gleam with the blood of purification."[27]

Like the Germans, they believed that they were a superior race. It has been said that the German soldier was trained to kill and the Japanese soldier was trained to die. One of the first lessons a Japanese soldier was taught was how to die, how to kill himself. It was shameful, cowardly, unpatriotic, to surrender. And of course the Japanese soldier was assured by his superiors that prisoners were tortured and butchered by the British and the Americans.

Anyone who ponders this question and wishes to compare it with the similar situation in Germany at the same historical time should read the book *Your Loyal and Loving Son* – Letters of Tank Gunner Karl Fuchs, edited and translated by Horst Fuchs Richardson. In a letter to his mother, in order to defuse a domestic argument, idealistic young Karl in his early twenties and an elementary school teacher, tells them that the worst thing in the world is hatred so his family must be peaceful towards one another. If only he could have applied those words to different nations, we wonder, but then we have to remember Fraser's words: "You must try to see the past in its own terms and values." In his own country, among his own people young Karl was a really good, moral citizen.

There were no Jews in the village where Karl grew up yet he absorbed the Nazi myths against the Jews and against any country that Germany attacked, firmly believing that he and his fellow soldiers were thereby saving Germany. Almost all his endearing letters to his mother, father and young wife ended with a "Heil Hitler".

Young Karl was killed in battle in 1941 near Moscow. If a fine young man like Karl Fuchs was influenced so fully by the leadership of his time, then there is no surprise at all that virtually the whole nation of Japan was fully influenced by its leadership.

On the wall of Bob's apartment is a brief visual depiction of the path that his part of the war took. There is a big white flag with a big red circle in its middle, given to Bob by another soldier. Every Japanese soldier had one compressed under his helmet. It was the national talisman that would keep him victorious and safe on the battlefield. Above the flag, placed like an X across each other, are two of the lethal Gurkha *kukri* weapons, many

---

[27] Lyrics from Japan's most popular song at that time, written by a navy lieutenant.

of which were also used by Indian and British soldiers in the latter part of the war.

LIEUTENANT JOHN PETTY

Remember Lieutenant John Petty, with whom Bob undertook that wonderful hike up the mountains near Darjeerling? Bob assumed that the lieutenant had been promoted early in Bob's time at the front and that's why he hardly saw him again. Well, Bob was right. The secretary of the military museum in Carlisle informed me that John Petty became a Captain and Acting Major, commanding B Company of the 9th Battalion Border regiment in 1945. On 10th of April 1945 he heroically led his company in an attack on the village Pyawbe, for which he was awarded the MC. He continued to serve after the War and retired a Lieutenant Colonel. His last job was Regimental Secretary of the King's Own Royal Border Regiment in Carlisle from 1975 to 1985. He died in 1995.

Lieutenant Colonel Petty's dress uniform was on display on a mannequin in the Carlisle Military Museum for a number of years with his medals and a Japanese sword he had captured. Without knowing this, Bob visited the museum one day and as he approached the figure of John Petty from the back he thought it was John Petty himself because the stature of the figure was exactly like the real John Petty. So, in a manner of speaking, Bob was pleased to encounter Lt Petty once more.

In Conclusion

One could say that Bob was a leader who suffered the consequences of his moral concepts. How do you reconcile the pain of experiencing the progressive shattering of your noble expectations of the calibre of your fellow men with your mission to play your part for your country in fighting an evil, world-threatening injustice? And on top of that discordant striving, to have to wade through the killing fields, as it were, in order to achieve that mission, is daunting in the extreme. For Bob to have shouldered all this through his four years of war experience and beyond it to this present day makes him a unique, singular, courageous man – a man alone.

One could also say that Bob retained an innocence into adulthood and that his war experiences did not blemish his singular character and helped to keep him on his straight path through life.

Generally, with Bob there were no half measures. If he had a clear, direct case of bad opposition to him, he took action alone, instantly as in the case of McGuire heckling him, or if he had to prepare for that action for a year, as in the case of the bully at school.

But in war conditions, subtle, underhand, unobtrusive opposition by a group was not something he could solve alone yet he believed it could not be solved any other way. So he had to compromise, be watchful and distance himself far enough from the problem so that he could at least get on with his determination to be a really effective soldier in the field.

His own conclusion after the war, in words he said to me, was: "I was better at carrying out orders than giving them."

To me this is sad, when you think of the army's initial high regard for him, expressed in their quick promotion of him to sergeant and when you think of his combat actions in the war. However, these words of Bob's suggest that he was perhaps aware that he lacked the sort of qualities that a good leader should have, qualities that would have enabled him to deal with his problem with his men or even to have prevented the problem from developing. Yet in the end we can be thankful that there can still be examples of people with high moral standards who will stick to them through thick and thin to the end.

What did nothing to improve Bob's dim view of the average British soldier was that, late in the war, two more soldiers were added to his platoon. Bob thought that they were either the survivors of a depleted platoon or were not wanted by any other part of the infantry. They were liars and thieves, Bob said, just looking after themselves.

With regard to the Japanese soldiers he killed – Bob believed he was fighting a war against evil, against a threat to the whole civilised world, and he stuck to his resolve as best he could on and off the field.

He told me that when he was in possession of a Tommy gun on one occasion deep in a bushy area, he was tempted to mow down the whole clique. He controlled that temptation quickly.

One would like to say that Fraser's section represented the core of the British infantry in the Burma war and that Bob's section was an exception to the rule. However, Bob's story reminds us that men are not all heroes just because they fought on "our" side in a war; they are still men with both their good points and their bad points and that the latter can endanger the lives of others.

Anyone who wishes to read the overall story of the Burma/India war from start to finish should read Field Marshal Sir William Slim's book *Defeat Into Victory*.

Anyone wishing to experience a wonderful sense of reconciliation and peace eventually stemming from this war should read *The Souvenir* by Louise Steinman.

Bob's Own Writing

Here follows two memories written by Bob himself. They illustrate what a good autobiography he would have written had he decided to do so earlier in his life. The pain of remembering those war-torn days was a reason why he did not do so (or speak about those years) for a long time. In fact he just wanted to blot out his whole war experience from his mind. Also, in later life the weakening of his eyesight put paid to his writing and reading. However, before his eyesight weakened too much, he wrote the following two pieces.

FRIENDLY FIRE by Bob Robinson (written in 2002)

When I saw the news on television that some Canadian soldiers had been killed by (American) friendly fire in Afghanistan, I did not sleep for some hours as my mind went back 60 years. Around the end of June 1942 we found ourselves stationed in Fort William in Calcutta, India which was our home for 11 months. Each move after this took us closer to the war in Burma in 1944 and 1945 and to face the Japanese Imperial Army.

We were an infantry regiment from Cumbria in the North of England. We were made part of the 9th infantry Battalion, Border regiment, a part of the 17th Indian Division. 90% of the officers and NCOs were regular soldiers who wore the green and black ribbon of the North-West Frontier of India. They spent a large part of their military life in this area and areas of the Kyber Pass.

The following are some of my experiences of "Friendly Fire".

We spent six days a week in training. Most of this was in the paddy fields on the outskirts of Calcutta. This one particular day was to be, for most of us, our "Baptism of Fire". We were lined up in rows and facing an "enemy" fortification 200 yards away. Three miles behind us were batteries of 25 pounder field guns of the Royal Artillery. The muzzle of every gun was pointed at us. This exercise is called a "creeping barrage" and it was a preparation for the real thing.

At a given signal you flatten out on the ground. At that instant you hear the thump, thump, thump of the guns opening fire. In three seconds those shells pass overhead with an ear-splitting scream and then there's an equally ear-splitting roar as they explode one hundred yards ahead of you. The firing stops, you advance and take over the position where the shells exploded, lay down, and the firing starts again, the muzzles of the big guns having been elevated one or two degrees. We were learning the purpose of our friendly fire: to destroy or soften up the enemy in preparation for the infantry to advance. The splinters of the exploding shells are about the size of your finger, jagged and red-hot. They tear into the flesh and cause nasty wounds or death.

The following day this friendly fire ended in disaster as one of the shells fell short and right onto the artillery's own observation post. Their Commanding Officer, second-in-command and several other officers were killed.

The second incident happened like this: we were part of the British forces that had taken Meiktila from the Japanese 50 miles south of Mandalay and were pushing down the road to Rangoon, cutting the Japanese army in two. Most of the villages situated in the paddy fields were held by Japanese forces, so it was our job to destroy them. The American "Flying Tigers" had offered to bomb one of these villages. These pilots were volunteers flying for the Chinese, to help the Chinese forces in their struggle against the Japanese. At this time a Chinese army with American officers was in fact working its way from North/West China down towards Mandalay.

These planes bombed a village close to us. All their bombs were on target except one. This massive bomb, about three feet across and five feet long landed and bounced, skidded and ground its way down a gentle slope towards us. It did not explode and finally came to rest in a gully in the middle of our position without harming anyone. Because of continued bombing, and enemy fire from the village, we spent an hour huddled around that thing. We couldn't take our eyes off it. We were glad to move on and put as much distance as possible between ourselves and that massive piece of death and destruction. It was a case of friendly fire that did us no harm, but gave us grey hairs.

In 1944 we had faced the Japanese in the Chin Hills for six months and at 9,000 feet – a situation where tanks cannot be used. But now in 1945 we were on the plains and we had the use of American "Sherman" tanks. We had taken one village and were on our way to the next village about a mile away. We passed about ten of these tanks lined up on the outskirts of the village and firing towards our objective. The tank shells did not have the ear-splitting shriek of the 25 pounders when they passed a few feet above our heads but they were bad enough. We had not gone very far on these bare flat fields when the enemy guns opened up and shells began falling among us. We had just received a new officer that morning. Within five minutes he was dead. He fell backwards into a three feet deep ditch just in front of me. I looked down at him with very mixed feelings but deaths like his had become part of the war's routine.

Two hundred yards from the village the enemy machine guns opened up. With the bullets hissing about your head, you stoop as low as you can and look for cover. We saw a short bund (low wall of earth) 150 yards from the village. We ran for it. The only drawback was that it placed us directly under the high explosive shells of our tanks. What we didn't know was that one of our companies was pinned down between the bund and the village.

Because of this, the tanks switched to smoke shells to form a smokescreen. It worked and that company was able to withdraw. At least most of them.

The bund gave us the protection we needed; it enabled us to catch our breath and have a drink of precious water. There were about twelve of us in that small area. We were fascinated by the smoke shells leaving the muzzles of the tank guns, leaving long trails of smoke overhead. We could not see the projectile, only the leading edge of the smoke.

Gun layers are human and like most of us can make mistakes. One degree in elevation to the low side can be devastating. I was looking at a shell leaving one of the tanks. This one was different. The trajectory was low and the shell was heading straight for the centre of my body. In a split second I saw a sudden and violent death approaching me at the speed of sound. One second was all it took for that 3 by 16 inch shell to fall 40 feet short, tear a 3 foot wide furrow in the baked mud, exit the ground 12 feet away and pass a few inches over my head. When the shower of dirt, dust and smoke had dispersed, I studied what had happened. It was as though a miracle had taken place.

The tanks' switching from high explosive shells to smoke shells saved the lives of all of us that day.

For the following 14 hours I was not "with it". I must have been like a zombie. I don't remember leaving the cover of the bund, I don't remember attacking the village over the last 150 yards or occupying the enemy trenches and positions. I don't recall digging a hole with my bayonet or using my hands as a shovel and then collapsing and lying there all night. Yet I did, the other members of the group assured me when I was eventually *compos mentis*.

The expected Japanese counter-attack never came, fortunately for me. Had I suffered a mild form of shell shock or just sheer exhaustion? We shall never know.

A few days later as we entered another village we were held up by enemy rifle and machine gun fire from a series of trenches and foxholes in the centre of the village itself.

"Friendly Fire" was called for. Three of us took cover behind a tree, standing one behind the other – a very foolish thing to do for we should have been spread-eagled on the ground. We heard the thump of the 25 pounders open fire and the high pitched scream of the shells as they passed a few feet over our heads and then the tremendous explosions as they impacted on target about 50 yards ahead.

We became careless and started peering round the tree, each time a little further out. Something made me turn round. The third man was clutching his shoulder, the torn clothing and blood. A shell splinter had come back, missed our faces by inches and taken a large piece of flesh from the top of his arm. That was the type of wound we all dreamed about, just to get away from that hell called Burma.

When the battle came to an end I walked over to that tree and relived those few minutes. I searched the area and found the piece of shrapnel. It was the size of my finger and full of jagged ridges. It was still warm and the barbecued flesh on it was so baked on it that I could not remove it.

I found the place where the wounded were lying on the ground, located the soldier and presented him with this ticket home.

Bob Robinson, *West Vancouver*

THE GOLDEN GRASS by Bob Robinson (2002)

Around September 1944 our final training in the military camp of Happy Valley in the outskirts of the Hill Station of Shillong, Assam, was over. We were now an infantry unit of the XIV Army. The convoy was over one mile in length and consisted of trucks only, our speed being about 10m.p.h.

Our final destination was the village of Tiddim in the Chin Hills of Manipur State and then on to Kennedy peak at 9,000 feet. We were to face the victorious Japanese 33rd Division and the leading units of the Japanese Army, then poised in readiness for the assault on India.

As we gradually gained elevation, the roads on which we were travelling were no more than tracks made by bullock carts over the centuries. There were many signs of improvement carried out by those unsung heroes the Indian Corps of engineers and sappers working entirely with pick and shovel.

We passed through every type of terrain imaginable: forests, jungle, flat and hilly areas, scrub, areas littered with rocks and others resembling a moonscape. At night we stopped and slept. by the side of the road.

After several days we hit a section that was different from anything we had seen. The road consisted of two lanes, flat and straight for several miles. It was an excellent place to stop for a breather and stretch our legs. The trucks pulled over to the right in the shade of the trees. As the men jumped out they all headed for the welcome shade after the confinement of the trucks.

For the last two or three miles I had been intrigued by what lay on the left of this road. A tall dark greenish brown forbidding looking hedge stretched for miles along the roadside. The lower eight feet looked so smooth and the whole thing so perfectly straight it was hard to believe it was a work of nature.

I walked over to the hedge and ran my hands over it. It was rough to the touch. This outside layer was six feet tall. It was so tightly woven I don't think a knife blade would have gone through. I pushed against it but there was no give. It was solid and impenetrable. The whole thing was about 12 feet high. I walked along the edge, looking for a flaw in the hedge and I suddenly found one. Taking a last look to right and left and seeing no-one, I fought my way into the hedge.

I know now it was a foolish thing to do. I was alone, no-one could see me. I had informed no-one of my intentions. We were also in quite a hostile environment.

Keeping my head down to protect my eyes and using my forearms, I pushed this heavy growth to the side. I was travelling in a dark and gloomy tunnel. I plunged ahead for about 20 paces until I realised there was no further resistance and I was in daylight.

I raised my head and all I could see was a huge mass of gold. The colour of pure gold in the form of over six feet tall grass. In twenty paces I had left

the real world and entered a fairyland, one of nature's works of art, something you may expect to find on another planet. I just stood there, trying to
take it all in and wondering, "Is there another place like this on earth?"

My entry had brought me into the centre of this semi-circle. It was like a
display area. Only one flaw broke the symmetry of the shorter grass. Here,
instead of rising in a slope, it butted into the stems of the long grass. The
exposed area, about nine feet high, showed the top half of the tall grass
formation. It was incredible to look at.

The 40 stems on display were equally spaced, four inches apart. These
were topped with seed heads similar to our meadow grasses, only much
larger. When inspecting these heads later, I could see that each head was
gently touched by four others. This made for a very dense growth.

In this whole area there was no movement and no sound. There was no
dust, no dirt, all was immaculate. There appeared to be no birds or insects
or any living thing.

I strode forward about forty paces until I was surrounded by the tall
grass. The grass hugged my body, the seed heads touched my face and
extended several inches above my head. Growing through the grass and
spaced about 8 feet apart were tall, slender saplings 24 feet in height. The
bark was pure white, there were no branches to be seen but each tree was
topped by a cluster of small bright green, shiny leaves.

Tilting my head back to its fullest extent, I could see a small patch of
blue sky overhead. I turned my attention to the seed heads in front of my
face; they were so beautifully formed, so intricate and delicate they re-
minded me of high quality lace.

Suddenly all this changed. I had been in there for too long. I had lost all
track of time and convoys never stop for very long. I could feel a panic
attack coming on and my imagination was running away with me. What if
I made one wrong move and became disoriented? What if the convoy had
moved on and I was left alone to face a night, miles from anywhere?

I suddenly felt very lonely in an environment that was becoming un-
friendly, even menacing. Those seed heads were looking at me with
unseeing eyes that said, "You could remain with us forever. No-one will
ever find you and you will in time become one of us."

I turned around carefully and without a glance back headed for the
hedge. My sense of direction was good and, after struggling through that
dense brush, I staggered through the opening and onto the road.

I can't put into words the relief I felt when I saw the trucks still there. No-one seemed to notice my bruised and bleeding forearms. If they did no-one mentioned it. No-one had missed me. But I held a secret that no other man in my regiment could even dream about and it was only 20 feet away.

As we slowly pulled away I followed the hedge with my eyes until it disappeared from view. What lay behind me and what I had seen and done in that short period of time are memories I have to this day. That golden grass, so tall, so fragile, so fascinating, so beautiful, so deadly.

Bob Robinson, *West Vancouver*

Comment by Peter Court:

In the first passage written by Bob we see the resilient man experiencing the hazards of an aspect of warfare – the often present danger of fire on the field from one's own side. Unfortunately for Bob the danger was also off the field.

The second passage reveals a Bob appreciative of and sensitive to his natural surroundings. It is also a metaphor of the individual man exploring, taking on life and its dangers while upholding his dignity and values. It could also suggest the lone young man's venturing forward with "golden" ideals and expectations which are then shadowed in the danger of solitary experience or isolation. There is a sense of wonder and sadness in the experience.

Last Thoughts

Although Bob had little regard for the common British soldier, he did appreciate the big picture of the war in India and Burma and its place in world history. Like me, he agrees with George McDonald Fraser's following words:

> "This was the last great battle in the last great war, with 'the scrapings of the barrel' from half the nations of the world (the Allies) fighting under one of the greatest Captains (Field Marshal Sir William Slim), in mountain, jungle, dry plain, in hot sun and drenching monsoons, and inflicting on one of the great warrior nations its most crushing defeat."[28]

It is interesting to note that the well-known Japanese film producer, Yamada Yogi, has said:

> "There are still not enough films being made about the massive tragedy of Japan's involvement in World War Two."

We can add to his call for more films, more books, biographies and where possible, autobiographies written about the experiences of the individual soldier in the war in every country attacked by the Japanese *and* the experiences of Japanese soldiers. Learning about a war as experienced by men on the spot is essential if you are to really understand that war.

For excellent reading of first hand participation in this war by an infantryman I recommend *The Little Men* by K.W. Cooper and *Quartered Safe Out Here* by George MacDonald Fraser. Equally gripping and heartfelt by a senior officer is John Master's *The Road Past Mandalay*, especially his time with the second Chindits expedition. For a first hand pilot's participation read *Young Man You'll Never Die* by Merton Naydler.

My last thought is of Field Marshal Sir William Slim's saying that an Army can be seen as an inverted pyramid with a broad base at the top and the whole balanced on a single fine point – the individual soldier. In time

---

[28] *Reproduced with the permission of Curtis Brown Group Ltd, London on behalf of The Estate of George MacDonald Fraser.

of war the family can be seen in a similar way, which brings to mind the epitaph on the gravestone of a young soldier in the Kohima cemetery:

To the world
Our Tom was just another soldier
But to us
He was the whole world.

~ End ~

Bob and Mayor of West Vancouver, Pam Goldsmith-Jones
at a World War Veterans' dinner in West Vancouver 2009.

Bibliography

Defeat into Victory by Field Marshal Sir William Slim.

The Campaign in Burma, Prepared for South East Asia Command by Central Office of Information, His Majesty's Stationery Office, London.

On to Rangoon, printed and published by G. Claridge and Co Ltd, Bombay, under the authority of the War Department, Government of India.

Nemesis by Max Hastings

All Hell Broke Loose by Max Hastings

Quartered Safe Out Here by George McDonald Fraser

Not Ordinary Men by John Colvin

We Gave Our Today by William Fowler

Forgotten Voices from Burma by Julian Thompson

Young Man, You'll Never Die by Merton Naydler

Your Loyal and Loving Son by Horst Fuchs Richardson

The Little Men by K.W. Cooper

Beyond the Chindwin by Bernard Ferguson

The Road Past Mandalay by John Masters

The Souvenir by Louise Steinman

Also by the author:
Hear the Ringdove Call (ISBN 978-1-920084-76-9) A novel set during the Siege of Ladysmith. Raven Press, South Africa.

Peter Court has also written a screenplay version of *Hear the Ringdove Call* and a screenplay version of *A Man Alone*.